# JANICE K

# Voices
# Galore

First Published in Great Britain 2016
by Twinlaw Publishing
Kirkcairn, Westruther, Gordon
Scottish Borders TD3 6NE

Revised reprint June 2016

The author acknowledges the spoken words of those she interviewed on Siar FM's Barra Island Discs, those words forming the basis of this book.

A CIP catalogue record for this title is available from the British Library

ISBN: 978-0-9932220-5-4

www.twinlawpublishing.co.uk

*Mum and Dad, Jessie and Rob Kielty, always x*

*The late Alex MacKenzie, the 'Bonach' of Glencoe who loved Barra and is sorely missed.*

*Curstaidh Peigi and Roddy MacLeod, true friends who taught us how to laugh in Gaidhlig! B' i sin reul's an oidhche dhoilleir...*

*And finally to the Barraich and those close to them who embraced the idea of Barra Island Discs and brought it to life. Abair ach beagan agus abair gu math e. Moran Taing ma tha.*

'To see the world in a Grain of Sand
And Heaven in a Wild Flower
Hold Infinity in the palm of your hand
And Eternity in an hour...'
**William Blake 1757–1827**

# Map of Barra

# About Janice Ross

Janice, her husband and three daughters.

Born in Hamilton and growing up in Whitlawburn, Cambuslang, Janice, between 1978 and 1981, attended the junior school at the Royal Scottish Academy of Music and Drama. She acted with some of the household names of Scottish television and theatre, but was way too tall to be an actress in Scotland – six feet. Her love of reading took her to the gates of Gilmorehill where height did not prevent her gaining an MA degree. After a year at Jordanhill, training to be an English teacher, she taught in Lanarkshire whilst completing a master's degree [MSc] and preparing a doctoral thesis on Equality and Discrimination. She then followed her forefathers into trade unionism, wrote articles for the *Scottish Educational Journal* and the *Times Educational Supplement* and embraced all that was good and just in life's struggle.

Holidays were spent with her husband and three daughters on the west coast, camping on Arran and at Arisaig and Morar. When her husband took a job in the Highlands, the family settled among the cool, clear, crisp mountain air of Glencoe, with the brooding majesty of Buchaille Etive Mhor on their doorstep.

When Janice agreed to cover a six month supply teaching post in Benbecula she later came to Barra and found her spiritual homeland. She loves Barra's landscape, the sea and island life.

After gaining a master's degree in Humanities [MRes] she is putting together a doctoral thesis on the art of blethering.

*Barra Island Discs*, her weekly radio show gave free rein to her penchant for hearing the blethers of others as she listened to the rise and fall of the voices of the island.

# About Voices Galore

Janice Ross
Barra Island Discs · Siar FM

Just what is a Barraich and what does it mean to be one?

Ever wondered what it is like to live on a small, remote and rural island community with the unforgiving Atlantic Ocean on the west side shore and the cruel Minch on the east side?

For the very first time in Scotland, this unique book presents a collection of voices from the small Hebridean islands of Barra and Vatersay as recorded on the community radio.

At the end of 2009, as a volunteer, I set up *Barra Island Discs*, a light entertainment programme for Siar FM. The main purpose of the hour long interview show was for the local community to hear itself and laugh at each other's life stories. Five years later, with over a fifth of the adult population recorded along with some others, what emerged was a rich tapestry of the cultural history of the community. Themes such as identity, community, family, employment and education, the golden threads of all our lives, are to be found in this text along with a fierce defence of the beautiful melodious Gaelic language spoken by the Barraich.

Since there are around 150 hours of interviews, making the selection has not been easy. Those in this book have been chosen because I think they helped to create my view of the island during the years the show has been running. They reflect its make up in terms of those who live here all year round, and those who come to seek out its abundant gifts.

*Voices Galore* presents the story of an island community at the beginning of the twenty first century as told by itself.

# Foreword: Angus B MacNeil MP

Janice Ross pulls together an interesting series of voices from her time in Barra giving a snapshot of people's views and experiences of Barra island life at that point in time. Doubtless there will be fun points, serious points and reflective points as well as many other points in the transformation from short radio programmes to an island life chronicle that Janice has pulled together.

Most notable to non-islanders will be an interview with Bob Crow, the late leader of the Rail and Maritime Union and someone who loved the Hebrides. He might have been known for his activism with trade unions and the railways but Bob was also well aware of the Maritime side of his job too. From my own perspective, doubtless there will be a laugh with what witty crofter Jimmy Ferguson has to say or the ever interesting perspectives of my former primary teacher Peggy MacCormick. And also DJ Wilson and James Davidson who were leading figures in the Barra Football team's very successful season in 2015. To be honest, all will be interesting, and will be interesting at different points again in the future as time moves on and the community changes.

This is a compelling use of oral testimonies which conveys the identity and cultural history of the island at this particular time. As far as I am aware this is the first time a book like this has been written in Scotland, it just proves how effective community radio can be in recording the life stories of us ordinary, everyday people. I commend the tome to the reader on many levels and I'm sure the overriding feeling will be one of interest and enjoyment of reading about island life here on Barra.

*Angus Brendan MacNeil MP*

# On Barra Island Discs

**Billy McNeill and Janice Ross**

"I certainly enjoyed my time on the programme and it enabled us both – she and me– to address a more knowing and intimate audience than a bigger broadcaster would allow. I hope these programmes are archived as they will also be a useful social history, beyond their original purpose, in years to come."
*Angus B MacNeil MP*

"I have not had any media experience. I have not been on the radio or television, so I was quite nervous about the prospect... On the day, the interview was conducted really nicely and calmly. Since I was well prepared I could relax and really enjoy the experience." *Jules Akel,* Graphic Designer

"...she [Janice] delivered a programme which in my opinion was much better and to a higher standard than many that I have heard and been involved with."
*Professor Sir William Stewart DSc, FRS*

"It provides a historic record of people's life experiences and an insight into the lives of the youth element within our community. It provides a unique service that brings the entire community together..." *Councillor Donald Manford*

"I do of course recall taking part in your Barra Island Discs programme and remember the positive response it received from constituents at the time. The format certainly has a contribution to make towards community engagement and, for my part, I would welcome its development and proliferation in wider communities." *Alasdair Allan MSP,* December 2011 – 18 May 2016 Scottish Government Minister for Learning, Science and Scotland's Languages, May 2016 Minister for International Development and Europe.

# Contents

Kisimul Castle    Copyright © AnnieM

Dedication
Map of Barra
About Janice Ross
About Voices Galore
Foreword: Angus B MacNeil MP
About Barra Island Discs

Chapter –

1. Chief, Comic, and the Campbell of Castlebay Bar
   *Rory MacNeil of Barra, Norman MacLean, John Campbell*
2. Crofter, Skipper, Holiday Tripper
   *Jimmy Ferguson, Seonaidh Beaton, Clare Brett*
3. Doctor, Dentist, Nurse
   *David Bickle, Robert McIntosh, Mairi a' Welder*
4. Barra's Burly Boys
   *Willie Douglas, Calum MacNeil, Donnie MacNeil*
5. Songbird, Storyteller, Poet
   *Mairi Mhol, Christopher Brookmyre, and Donald Murray*
6. Priest, Spark, Trade Union Bark
   *Father John Paul MacKinnon, Hec MacLean, Bob Crow*
7. Teacher, Councillor, Minister
   *Peggy MacCormick, Donald Manford, Alasdair Allan*
8. Projectionist, Activist, Scientist
   *Iain McColl, Christine Galbraith, Professor Sir William Stewart*
9. Young, Daring, Bold
   *Deege Wilson, Catriona Nicholson, James Davidson*
10. Midwife, Mother, Matriarch
    *Nellie MacArthur, Nanag Gillies, Patsy Buchanan*
    Afterword
    Acknowledgements

CHAPTER ONE

# Chief, Comic and the Campbell of Castlebay Bar

# Rory MacNeil of Barra

*Interviewed 16.08.10*

Assuming responsibility of chief of the clan MacNeil, Rory, the MacNeil of Barra, spoke to me just a few months after his father's death. This is his story.

"I guess it is mixed emotions really, it is a responsibility obviously and it's an even bigger responsibility because of the way my father fulfilled the role, and they are big shoes to follow but on the other hand it is a way of being involved in the Barra community, and for people who know the Barra community, it is a fantastic opportunity. It is a wonderful community to have a chance to be involved with and I have been involved with it before for many years, but this perhaps is a way of deepening the involvement so I view that as great.

Everyone has been so kind. At the funeral in February the community came out in a way which was wonderful and everyone has been very, very nice to my mother.

I grew up in upstate New York. The first time I was in Barra was in 1965. We were on our way between New York and Tanzania. My dad was going to teach law there and we made a side trip here – or dad and I made a side trip up to Barra. We stayed at the Craigard Hotel and my first impression of Barra was perhaps not a very normal one because my dad had been here in the thirties as a boy and because through him and his father he knew a lot of people on Barra. In 1965 a lot of the people he knew were getting old, and my impression as a ten year old was we went to visit a lot of old ladies who talked about the people who had died. It was a bit surreal, and only a couple of days as well.

Well, we took the boat – the *New Amsterdam* it was – and it was with the Hull American Line, from New York to Southampton. That was an incredible adventure for a ten year old. It made a huge impression on me. I will tell you a little anecdote mostly about my father. An incredible coincidence happened. My best friend from school happened to be on the boat, and I don't think we even discovered it until we were on the boat. It was great because we had all day to play together, and every evening there was bingo. One evening my friend, I think he was playing every evening, but this evening I was allowed to stay up and play bingo and the two of us were sharing a card. I think it cost a dollar to play the bingo, so we played a few games and didn't win so dad said, 'Rory, come on, it is time for you to go to bed,' and I said, 'Oh no.' He said, 'No, it is time for you to go to bed,' but my friend Jim got to stay up and play, and the next game he won. We had a great time on the boat. It was fantastic."

Visiting far flung countries has always been part of Rory MacNeil of Barra's life. As they say, travel broadens the mind.

"I have been around, I guess. I spent a lot of time in East Asia and I taught English in Japan after university, that was my first experience with East Asia. I was going to get a PhD in Chinese History, and in conjunction with that I lived in Taiwan for two years and learned Mandarin. Then I decided I was not cut out to be a Chinese scholar, so I went back to the States and got my law degree. That was in the mid eighties when China was beginning to open up and so I practised law briefly in San Francisco then I went out to Beijing and ended up spending sixteen years in Hong Kong. So yes, I spent time mostly in the Far East and it has been a very international experience.

I speak Mandarin not perfectly but I can certainly hold a good conversation in Mandarin."

Rory, MacNeil of Barra, speaking to the largely Gaelic speaking audience in Mandarin said, "Hi everyone, the weather is not too good today but I hope everyone has a good day."

"I think it is very useful to speak Mandarin. China is a huge place of course, a very diverse place, and Mandarin is the lingo to some extent. It certainly helped me get around China and do business in China. I don't do business anymore in China now particularly, but I occasionally run into Chinese people and it is useful there. Both of my sons are learning Mandarin at school, which is nice as well. So we are hoping they will also be able to use Mandarin when they grow up."

On Gaelic he said, "Chan eil, uisge, tha gu math. Yes I am learning. It is one of the languages I am studying in Edinburgh. One of the difficulties is who you are speaking with, and it depends on their dialect. What you want is the Barra dialect. But I am pleased to say I am studying at a class in Edinburgh and three of the group have Barra connections, so we now dominate the class. So that is good news."

His Gaelic may not be as good as it could be, but his feet move nimbly around the ceilidh floor.

"Everyone knows I like dancing. The second time I came to Barra was in 1971 when we came for the whole summer. I was sixteen. So among other things, I discovered the Barra dances. In those days, I don't know if my memory serves and I don't know if it is true, but it seemed there was a lot more dances. It seemed that there was two to three dances every week – that was my impression anyway. I learned the dances, and I love the songs as well, and ever since then I loved what I call the Barra dancing. Actually in Berkeley in California, when I was a graduate student there, I learned proper Scottish country dancing which I also like, but of course that is not the same as the real thing they do in Vatersay Hall. However I am a terrible singer so I can't sing at ceilidhs, but try keeping me off the dance floor."

Kisimul Castle, home to Rory MacNeil of Barra, sits brooding in Castlebay and I wondered if he, his wife and two sons lived there.

**Rory MacNeil of Barra with Kisimul Castle, his family home, in the background.**

"We used to live in the castle – until about 1991 or about 1992 – but the castle…it is a fantastic place but it is also quite isolating. It is quite hard to live there because you have to take all your things back and forth by boat and bring your rubbish in, and when the weather is bad you might just get stuck out there. People can't just pop in and say hi, you have got to arrange visits and things like that, so for a variety of reasons my parents thought it would be really nice to have a place onshore, and Dullach was kind enough to decroft a house site for us which took in the ruin of an old house, and we built a new house in and around that. It is up in Garrygall.

But the castle is a great place and if you spend a lot of time in it you develop affection for it as a place with all the nooks and crannies and rocks and the interesting features. It is interesting how it grows on you. In fact, I must have been stimulated by my early visits to it, because I am interested in castles, you know. If a place has a castle I always want to visit it, so I think it rubs off on you in various ways."

The MacNeil Gathering has proven to be very successful and was well underway when we were chatting.

"Well, it has been great and this format we are using now – I think it is the third time we have used it – is really good. There was a large gathering in 1977, 87 and 97. The one in 97 there was almost three hundred people here and all of those were organised by overseas agents. My father thought it would be better if the gatherings were organised locally for a couple of reasons. Firstly, because the visitors would be more involved with local Barra people. And he wanted more flexibility in the programme. If you organise it from overseas you have to have it organised and paid for in advance, whereas if it was done locally then you can have more flexibility in the programme. It has been really successful. I said on Monday at the opening session that my two objectives for the visit – and no doubt they had their own – was for them to get to know Barra people and to get to know each other. We had a dinner last night, and I think my objectives were fulfilled. Sarah MacLean has organised all three. She does just a fantastic job and makes everyone welcome. I think it was great.

I think for me the highlight – certainly it was the most dramatic moment – was *Trouble on the Croft*, the play, drama, – that was fantastic, but I think different people had different highlights. A lot of people mentioned Calum's talk on genealogy. That was fantastic, and we had a reception out at the castle. That was good. We had an opening session where Donald Manford and Ruraidh a' Butcher and my brother Sandy talked about their memories of my father and his relationship with Barra. The reason I organised that was I tried to get people to see not just the tourists but a bit more of what Barra was really like, and that was successful.

People are talking about coming back to the next one so it must have been good.

I love the football games on the island. Barra FC are going from strength to strength. It reminds me of our first extended visit in 1971, because we lived over in Horve and I used to spend a lot of time on the football pitch, but never mind that's another story. No, but I love watching the football team. I have a group in Edinburgh. We call ourselves *FC Galleon*, just a bunch of old men, well mostly. A couple of younger ones, but mostly old men like me. In 2004 we made our first tour to Barra to play the Barra team. It was a great experience and the guys from Edinburgh just loved it. We came in from Edinburgh on the plane and landed on the beach. We had one game and plenty more other activities, most of which involved the bars. We lost 7-3, but I am pleased to say the next spring there was a rematch in Edinburgh and we at least managed an honourable draw in that one.

One of my favourite books is *Calum's Road*[1]. I read the book and I think many people read it because of what he did. It is an astonishing testament to individual will, and really the kind of epitome of what people on the islands do to survive, and have to do to survive. Most don't have to build roads, of course, but the resourcefulness and the commitment to getting something practicable done, as well as the commitment to – in the end – to try and save the culture and tradition. It is all those things and it is very inspirational. At the same time, it is incredibly depressing, and the sub theme which I was particularly interested in was fighting against the bureaucracy and how incredibly intransigent and heartless the bureaucracy was in grinding down Calum and the community. One of the things I tried to do – God I am delivering a lecture here, and I do apologise for that – but one of the things I tried to bring to the visitors of Barra is I tried to give them more than a superficial understanding of what goes on here. As we all know, Barra exists on a fairly fragile balance. In particular the transport links need to be improved, both the ferry and air service. I have been involved in those issues for a number of years, and I think the threat of establishment of the SACs[2] which is currently hanging over us, is an example of another form of bureaucracy gone mad. It is an example of the lack of

---

[1] This book is about one man's steely determination to build a road to his township on Raasay, an island off the coast of the Isle of in Skye, in the hope that more people would come. He did this by wielding a pick axe and turned his vision into a reality.

[2] SAC is a designated Special Area of Conservation. This refers to the Sound of Barra being named as such an area. It created huge tensions in the local community and a campaign group SHAMED [Southern Hebrides Against Marine Environmental Designations] led by Angus Macleod, a crofterfisherman from Eoligarry insisted decisions relating to the management of the area should involve the community so as to safeguard the fragility of the local island economies, heavily reliant on the bounty of the sea for their livelihoods.

bureaucratic support, and secondly an example of bureaucratic interference. So the kind of battles that many people in Barra are involved with are issues like that, I think, which resonate very strongly with Calum. He's an inspiration, but at the same time it is a reminder that often you don't win the battles. Hopefully, because in this case we have the whole community, and because it is not a dying community, we will win the battle. But it is unfortunate that the battles continue to have to be fought."

The great thief time with its plundering hands was stealing the minutes from us, and my conversation with Rory, MacNeil of Barra had to end. He finished off with the following.

"I remember the summer of 1971 – there wasn't a causeway then – and I remember going over to a dance in Vatersay Hall and that was fantastic. I remember coming back in the boat at about three o'clock in the morning. It was really beautiful. All of a sudden all the energy, noise and music of the dance had gone and everyone had calmed and quietened down. That's one of my favourite memories of being a Barra boy.

Donnie MacNeil coming back to Barra and Vatersay has had a massive influence on the island. You can't imagine Barra and Vatersay without The Vatersay Boys, and you can't imagine life without The Vatersay Boys. They are so unique and creative. That's another thing about Barra, they are not going to be just another piper, another accordion player, they are going to do something of their own and they have certainly done that in a way that is wonderful."

Rory MacNeil of Barra wears his father's shoes well and will walk many a mile in them.

# Norman MacLean

*Interviewed on 22.12.10*

Norman MacLean is a giant in the Gaelic community. I set out to meet him on a freezing cold December afternoon shortly after reading the first part of his autobiography, *The Leper's Bell*. Tinkling melodies and silvery words slipped effortlessly from his tongue into a melting pot of laughter. This is his story.

"Diamar a tha a h-uile daoine Bharraigh? How is everyone on Barra?

That's me sooking up to the Barraichs. I have a soft spot for Barra. I don't have any connection with it, but I still have a lot of friends in Barra and a lot of people I owe money to – but I won't go into that. Nice people, and this is me ingratiating myself with them. I don't know what I am going to be speaking about today, I am just putty in your hands.

My Barra friends are the former headmaster of Castlebay School [the late] John Campbell, slightly older than myself, and in my opinion the best Gaelic speaker on the planet today. I have never heard Gaelic like it. Another person I went to university with is Ruraidh Pheiter, Roddy Campbell, who I believe has a croft in Glen now. That must be where his people were from because I know that Alan Johnstone and Calum Johnstone were related to him. Anyway, Roddy and I spent a misspent youth in the [Students'] union in Glasgow way back when. There are other people I know; there is a girl Flora Gillies from Vatersay that I know of, and I have a great pal from Vatersay. This is a guy with loads of money, and his name is Mick MacNeil, brother of Donnie MacNeil of The Vatersay Boys. Now let's put Donnie on the back burner because he is eccentric to say the least. I like Donnie, and I stayed with him for one weekend in Nasg. At that time he had no running water, no electricity. His sole heat source was candles, you know, but it made me a better man I think. But this is Donnie's brother Mick, another half breed like myself. His mother was Morag from South Uist, and his father was Uilleam Beag from Barra. Mick has bought himself a house in Vatersay. I think I was in it when it was being built, but it was dark that night – we had been to the hotel – but by now I am sure it will have three stories and a plantation portico – you know, a gallery full of sculptures. Nice guy Mick very, very good and he does a very inauthentic Gaelic accent, 'Jimmi ha ha hu and that, you aw right?' He is very, very funny and very, very talented. I am looking forward to seeing them all again, that's if the sun ever shines again.

I used to know Barra very, very well. I went over with Ruraidh Pheiter in 1958, in the Easter. What was happening then was an Ealing comedy, *Rockets Galore,* starring Jeannie something-or-other and Donald Sinden. Now I thought this was...you know, the Barra boys are really keen on nicknames, and for a full week I was under the distinct impression that Donald Sinden came from Cuithir or from Brevig or something, that he was just another of the boys, but no, he was a film star. All the young guys were getting jobs as extras, but Roddy and I were too young. But the guys older than us got jobs and boosted the takings for take-a-ways, but it was very good fun. That was my introduction to Barra and Barra society. And then love reared its head, and I started courting a woman from Brevig. I was hanging about there until they found out about me, and then I was extradited to the other end of the island.

In the late seventies a comely lass from Barra stole my heart. I saw her at the Feis recently – I was staying with the Maguires down in Horve. She was still looking fabulous and has a lovely house in Ledaig. I always think of her. I will come to Barra in the spring."

Eyes twinkling, only the blanket of snow outside the window cooled him down and he then went on to describe his life.

"The weather today would be a home from home for Captain Oates or Roald Amundsen, one of these old guys. All you needed in my bedroom this morning was a side of beef; it was a freezer I was in. It is very, very cold. I have on the long johns and the Damart thermals. I live with the Townsends and they have been very good to me, Peigi spoils me. The Townsends have been remarkably good to me.

I do have a house in Daliburgh which is about as handy as having a house in St. Petersburg. I think they are trying to maybe get me to move to North Uist. I was never in North Uist. My mother was from there, and my grandmother's people, but I don't know it all that well. I certainly know the fleshpots of Balivanich, and cut a swathe through that part of world, and I know Iodchar pretty well. I go to Respite Care in Daliburgh and that is fun, everyone shouting at the same time, it is great actually. I love the carers and my girlfriends. Mairi Gordon, who is about ninety six, is picked up by the chauffeur every morning, and Cathy Robertson. There is an old man from Garrymonie called Sammy MacPhee and he comes in at Christmas and New Year. It is a cheery place.

I am writing wee accounts of my life. I am having a good time. I went to see an English language pantomime performed by the Uist drama group and the Christmas concert of Sgoil Lionacleit, and then one at Paible School which was the best of the three nights. I was sitting as a fan and there were two young children Declan MacLennan and Karine MacLeod and Mairi McCorkindale, from Sollas I think, beautiful Gaelic. Unfortunately her Gaelic will be lost as she will become more Anglo centric. I had gone to the rehearsal at Paible, and what a shambles. I told Peigi that there were too many directors, and I told her to listen to me, Ridley Scott! But the mutual aid thing weaves together into a narrative arc and it all came together beautifully. I wrote and was in *Jack in the Beanstalk* in Inverness, and you had to speak in rhyming couplets. I think I could be called the first Hebridean rapper.

I have had a fairly long trajectory, so I have been about.

People said when I was thirty I wouldn't last. I am a classic cultural schizophrenic; I vacillate between the Gaelic and Govan. Other times it is modified Clydeside, because, like you, we have been to the degree factory. I have lived everywhere in Scotland. I have always been out and about looking for good looking women."

**Norman MacLean**  Copyright © Peigi Townsend

His book has been a real success and he hasn't looked back and of that he said, "Birlinn were a bit too conservative in ordering. It was launched in 2009, and at the national college of piping the evening was louping. I did a few readings and had it timed well and I signed copies for about two hours. We sold out, and when the Mod was in Oban I did five afternoon sessions and we sold out. By Christmas time all the hard back editions had sold out. Then there was a hiatus. It was great, they sent me a lovely cheque…I was very grateful. I trust that it is still going really well. I am hoping that the trilogy will be well received even though it will include some dark undertones.

The journey of my life includes dark periods. My wife, Peigi, – she is in Oban – she tells me the creator is keeping me for something, and I do believe there is a purpose in my endurance. I don't know. I used to wish for the heart attack but it didn't happen, and I came out of hospital nine months ago nicotine and alcohol free. That's the way it has to be.

I may plan to go Hong Kong to see my daughter. She has no bitterness, which will sustain me through this bitter winter, and I would love to go back to Mexico. It is such a death trap for me with alcohol – eighteen pence a bottle – and all these dusky maidens. They lied to me at school because Bill my geography teacher, he was a former Scotland rugby star, a hatchet man for the heidie, used to say when you get to South America all the women are ugly, they must have been ugly kids in their pram. He lied, they are gorgeous. The Mexicans had a dignity which was amazing, and when you cross the border you are on a different planet. The yanks are really slow compared to Mexico. America would grind to a halt without them.

Copyright © Norman MacLean

I won a gold medal for poetry and for piping. My wife wasn't happy with the amount of time I was spending. It wasn't her idea of being newly married, practising the pipes all the time and trying to get a pipe band together. I was teaching in Garthamlock [Glasgow], a real sin bin at the time, and I used to practise at lunchtimes. I was really prepared so it was a doddle and I enjoyed that, but when I started doing stand up I lost my voice, my range has gone."

Norman MacLean, Cuinnich, Loch Arkaig, 1956. Norman is possibly the only person in history to have won two gold Mod medals in the same year – one for piping, the other for poetry.

With forty miles of snow-covered roads and a ferry to catch I had to leave, but before I did Norman held me with his eyes and continued.

"Here's a couple of gags. A cailleach phoned up the Stornoway Gazette and asked to put in a death notice. The girl on the other end of the phone told her it would be £5 and asked what words she wanted. The caileach responded, 'Domhnall Macleod is dead.' 'That's a bit stark, Mrs McIver. You can add more for your £5.' The caileach's response was this, 'Okay, put this down. Domhnall MacLeod is dead. Tractor for sale.'

A bodach from Griminsh in Benbecula wants to buy a cow and he goes to a fair in Benbecula and there is a guy selling cows. The guy tells him, 'There are two choices I have a cow from Lochmaddy, she will be a great investment. She will give you a herd in about twenty years. Costs a bit more mind you, she is about a hundred guineas. I have another cow here from Lochboisdale. It is a lot cheaper, ten guineas, but it will only give birth once.' The old bodach, who didn't have much money, went for the cheap option. Right and true enough the cow gave him a calf then never again. He didn't know what to do, so he went to see an old man in Benbecula who knew about such things and he told this to the old man, 'I have a problem here. I have a cow that I paid £10 for, and the thing is, she has calved once but she wont let the bull near her. As soon as I bring the bull over she refuses to be served and kicks her legs and everything'. The old man asked if it had come from Lochboisdale and the bodach said, 'You are right. How did you know it came from Lochboisdale?' And the old man retorted, 'My wife is from Lochboisdale!'"

The snow covered road didn't make the car skid but the rip-roaring laughter did.

Moran Taing Tormod tha thu bodach uabhasach math.

Rainbow over water at Cleat beach

# Campbell of Castlebay Bar

*Interviewed on 05.05.11*

**John Campbell**

John Campbell is manager of Castlebay Hotel bar. He is married to Flora and father to Martin, John Archie and Andy. Martin joins his dad serving pints, John Archie is skipper on the Caledonian MacBrayne, Lochmaddy to Uig run, and Andy is currently training to be skipper. At the time of the interview John was preparing for an island invasion because of the success of *Island Parish*.[1] His dad makes daily trips to Mingulay during the summer season.

"I am from Barra. I am born and bred on Barra. There is an increase in the demand for accommodation on the island. The demand is very good for us and the whole of the Western Isles as everyone will benefit from it.

Castlebay Hotel is the oldest hotel on the island. It opened in 1860 for paying guests, so it has been there quite a while. It gets hard sometimes, but I have a good team beside me so it makes a big difference. We keep a record of all the guests who stay in the hotel. Quite a few famous people have stayed in the hotel and passed through, not in the past couple of years mind you, but there have been a few years I have met a lot of very nice important people.

Leslie Thomas the author, who wrote *Virgin Soldiers*. When you see people like Leslie Thomas you expect to see a six foot man. Leslie Thomas is very small, only about five feet two, and your impression is of someone completely different. Recently we

---

[1] *Island Parish* was a BBC programme created in 2011, providing a fly on the wall documentary style of the roles Catholic priests play in their community. It was filmed in the parishes of Barra, Eriskay and South Uist and became so massively popular that people were coming to the island to meet up with the local priests on the islands.

had Prince Charles, who was in the hotel a couple of times, and Princess Diana was in the hotel. They were just using it as a stop off point when they were up opening the school, right enough, but I met them. You bow your head just a wee bit and just shake their hands and that's it. So they are just ordinary people.like everyone else.

We are part of the island, so people see Castlebay as a reflection of how Barra is as an island as a whole.

Sometimes it is quite difficult. You have your hard times and the long hours so that you get tired, everybody gets tired. It is just a way of life. You just get on with it and knuckle down, and just remember the lovely guests and that. Even if there is someone famous we treat them just like every other person.

Well, I think Barra people treat everybody the same. What you see is what you get from a Barra person. Most Barra people accept everyone. They will talk to people, anybody that comes into the public bar in Castlebay, they will always talk to them. They will always offer them a drink. I have noticed that through the years, I have noticed that in the bar – not so much the hotel because it is a different place – but in the bar it is completely different. People accept them into the bar, and people want to know where they come from. In the last fifteen to twenty years when it was the old boys, the merchant seamen who had visited a lot of places, they would know where almost everyone came from. Most of the Barra folk who have been to sea have been all over the world.

When we used to have dances in the bar, Blair Douglas used to play in the bar when it was the only place open to one in the morning. I love his tune *Kate Martin's Waltz*. The bar was busy then, and Iain McLaughlin, Blair Douglas, the Walkmore Ceilidh Band and many more bands like the Tom Sloss Band, Ian McCorkindale, even Adam Scott, used to play there. Many of them are no longer with us, but they were great nights.

I have had a tune named after me, a pipe tune, but that is another story. It was a pipe tune that was written for me by Iain Joseph MacDonald from Spean Bridge, so that's a few years ago.

Campbell of
Castlebay Bar
at St. Kilda –
another of
his favourite
places.

Iain Joseph is a prodigy of Fergie MacDonald, the box player himself. Iain Joseph, he comes up to Barra himself now and again. He is a fantastic comedian along with being a box player. He can do Fergie MacDonald better than Fergie can do. No, I can't play. I couldn't play a box, nothing at all, not musical at all. I think there are certain families that are very musical, I think it follows the tradition. None of my family are musical except my brother Lye, he is musical now and again. He's a really good singer, or so he thinks.

The youngsters of Barra do very well for themselves and they are a credit to the island. They all tend to work at the hotel. We have fifteen rooms in the hotel. Just a mixture of twins, doubles and singles, and we have the nice MacNeil room which overlooks the bay. Many Barra people have stayed there. Honeymoon couples have stayed there. It is nice overlooking the castle and that. It is just one of these things."

His family is such a big part of John's life.

"My family is my wife Flora. She works in the canteen at Eoligarry School and she is a cleaner in Castlebay. She does a wee bit of running to keep fit. She wouldn't say that herself because she would like to be a lot fitter, but she will get there. I should do a lot more running and keep off the cream cakes but I can't. Yes she is a lovely baker, too good…she makes lovely puddings and that…I like homemade puddings and that. I like her cheesecakes, she makes lovely cheesecakes and banoffi pie and sticky toffee pudding. Flora has passed it on to her three boys and they can all cook, especially Andrew, but he is good at baking too. He is good in the galley.

Andrew is a merchant seaman. He is working out abroad most of the time. He flies out next week to Singapore for about nine weeks, so he will be sunning himself out there, working away. He's training to be a deck officer, well he is a deck officer now. He is sailing second mate just now with Squire Pacific. Martin works away there in the co-operative trying to do everything for everybody – get me this Martin, get me that Martin. John Archie, he works with CalMac. He is chief officer with CalMac just now. I think he is flying out to Poland today to join the new *Finlaggan*,[2] the new Islay boat. I don't know when she will be due to arrive in Britain, I think in a couple of weeks' time, so he is away out there doing final preparations.

Both their grandparents, their grandfathers, were seamen. It is a Barra thing all these seamen. It is a good thing for the boys being seamen. It is a good way of life. I wish I had been a seaman. I didn't do it because – I think it was partly at the time when I was leaving school – the merchant navy started taking boys from the inner cities, and not concentrating about the island so much. They brought in boys from the Glasgow area, but they found that the Glasgow boys didn't have the want for the sea. Then they came back to the island. These boys know they have to make a living, and the sea is a good living. It is a good way of life. Well, I think it is a good way of life.

All the islands as a whole, right through the Western Isles, benefit from the sea. You meet people that have been seafarers

---

[2] *Finlaggan* was a new vessel bought by Caledonian MacBrayne, the ferry company that covers the Scottish west coast. It was brand new and long over-due. John's son John Archie was appointed to be skipper of the new boat.

and some of them have been coming down to the hotel. Lately I have had three or four from Lewis coming down because the island infrastructure is good, the roads are good. It used to take you three or four days to come down, but now you can do it in half a day which is a great bonus for us all.

My nephew Iain Ruraidh and John Archie and Andrew, they were with my father and that, doing the Mingulay boat trips. They have learnt a lot from my father, learning to tie knots and boat handling skills, and now all these boys are merchant seamen today.

In the last couple of years when the boys have been away, I have been going up with my dad to Mingulay. It is the most tranquil place I have ever been to. You can be there and maybe there is a load of climbers up and two boats were there at the time – John Allan and the *Sollas* and the *Allasdale Lass,* and I would go ashore and help my dad laying out the boat. You could sit at the shore and you would think you were there by yourself it was that tranquil.

**Mingulay**

If you can go to Mingulay go. It is just gorgeous. Take a trip up there. You will be amazed.

I tell some of the people who come into the bar about Mingulay. I give them a wee bit of insight, like when the last people came off Mingulay, in 1912. Some went to Sandray then they went to Vatersay, the old village down at the shore in Vatersay and a lot of people go and do the old walk. You try and point the visitors to many things like the toffee factory, the heritage centre, to the airport to watch the plane coming in. A lot of people buy trips to land on the beach as anniversary presents and birthday presents, a fiftieth or sixtieth birthday present, ticking off the boxes as they go along.

I am a Gaelic speaker, a native Gaelic speaker. I try and speak it as often as I can, mostly to the people around me who have the Gaelic. Most of the team in the bar they understand it and there are a few who speak it. Well, I speak it to some of the guests: 'Madainn mhath', 'Feasgar math', and they try to speak it too. Even last night I was saying, 'Oidche mhath', to one of our guests, and she was trying it. But it was strange, she couldn't get her tongue around it. 'Madainn mhath', she could get perfectly well, but the 'Oidche', she couldn't pronounce it.

Well, the visitors I think they like it. They ask you to speak again. You think you are speaking normal until you hear yourself and you think that's not me speaking, but they like the lilt, the softness of the language. Well, I won't know because we all speak the same.

Most Saturdays when The Vatersay Boys are around it is very busy. They were away last weekend in Dingle Bay in Ireland, so they had a nice time. They are playing this Saturday night. I really like the boys, they are characters. They have been playing in the bar for a long time now. It is incredible the sound they have got. I think they were the start of all these up and coming young bands coming through.

When The Vatersay Boys are playing it is very busy, standing room only. The boys are great, I have heard them play that often, so many times, I used to close my ears off to them. They are characters, the boys, and they do pretty well for themselves. They are great entertainers.

I have been in Barra most of my life, I haven't been away yet, but there is always time for another adventure. There is still plenty of time. Could I just say thanks very much for all the help everyone has given me over the years, and that I miss the old seamen who are gone now, and I love the ones who are still here in the public bar who I serve with a half and a half [pint]."

There is never any trouble at the Castlebay Bar. With John Campbell at the helm it is easy to understand why.

CHAPTER TWO

# Crofter, Skipper, Holiday tripper

# Crofter

*Interviewed on 08.03.12*

**Jimmy Ferguson**

Jimmy Ferguson has a tawny brown weather-beaten face and eyes that sparkle like sun rays piercing the waves. Jimmy is married to Mary Ann and has three lovely daughters, Sarah, Jessica and Norma and his son, Alexander, affectionately known as Sandy. Born in Oban and brought up on the west side of the island in the township of Borve, Jimmy lives now just six hundred yards from his childhood home. He is a fluent Gaelic speaker. He spends all his free time crofting – out tending his sheep on the hills, growing potatoes and maintaining his lovely new house. His crofting skills were filmed for *Island Parish*[1].

This is what he says.

"Well they spent a couple of days filming but sadly it didn't get any airing at all, well I was quite looking forward to seeing myself and the wee man [his son Sandy]. I was hoping for film contracts to follow but sadly…lol. I have had cattle and sheep for a long while…this is my crofting poem by William McGonagall. Do you want to hear it?

*On yonder hill there was a coo but it is no there noo,*
*it must have moved…*

I know that is the case, you see it standing up a hill, you go up and the rascal has moved…lol!"

---

[1] *Island Parish* was a BBC programme created in 2011 providing a fly on the wall documentary style of the roles Catholic priests play in their community. It was filmed in the parishes of Barra and South Uist and became so massively popular that people were coming to the island to meet up with crofters and the local priests on the islands.

Jimmy's conversation is peppered with deliciously funny quips. His humour masks the very real knowledge he has of the sheep on the island and the wool they carry on their backs. When asked if crofters send the wool off to be returned for hand knitting, here is what he said.

"Some people used to do that, those who had the Jacob, and they will do if it is Hebridean sheep they keep, but the type of sheep I have means the wool gets sent away in a big bag to the mainland. We get paid per bag, so to be really honest, for a while it wasn't really worth much, but in the last year or two it has been worth quite a bit. Hopefully this year as the price of wool has gone up, it will be worth quite a bit. I have mostly Black face and White face with some Cheviots and the odd Suffolk. The difference between the Jacob and the Hebridean wool is the wool seems to be finer and black in colour, but most of the sheep on the island are texel cross and there is good money in them. Crofting in general means you need to look after the animals, you need to have a feel for it, you need to enjoy it and know that going out in all weathers is just part of it…you still enjoy it. I had cattle and pigs, but the feed stuff was so expensive they are now gone, and there is no dairy cows on the land, maybe there was years ago but not during my time…all the cattle now are for beef and breeding calves."

Jimmy Ferguson

When I pressed Jimmy about being multi-talented he said this.

"Like most of the people on the island, you have to be able to do a few things…"

At the time of the interview, one of Jimmy's jobs was to sell fish from the Barratlantic van in the Square at Castlebay. Every Thursday morning the most successful fish seller this side of the Minch would unashamedly flirt with his customers. You could step up to the van looking to buy a couple of slices of cod and come away with a heavy parcel of monk fish, salmon and lemon sole, descending the steps a few quid lighter. His silver tongued patter is as fresh as the fish he sells. What he doesn't know about island life isn't worth knowing. It is as simple as that.

Jimmy now works as one of two security officers at the airport. I can't think of anyone more suited to be an ambassador for the island.

Copyright © Janice Ross

**Barra landscape**

# Skipper

*Interviewed on 17.01.12*

Seonaidh Beaton is 81 years old. Recently widowed, he is father to two daughters and is a grandfather. Seonaidh's family came to Barra from South Uist, and he grew up with one sister and three brothers (they all became seamen). He is the only one left.

He owns and operates *Ocean View* a beautiful bed and breakfast establishment which looks across the machair of Borve into the pounding waves of the Atlantic Ocean. He is a piper, a crofter, and is one of the island's few taxi drivers. He is also a retired mariner.

Heading off like Sinbad to make his fortune sailing the seven seas, Seonaidh left his home in Borve at the age of fifteen, possessing two key qualities: knowledge of ancient mariner skills (much sought after by shipping companies both at home and abroad) and a keen sense of adventure.

This is what he says.

"I spent forty nine years at sea…well in my young days all the young lads headed for the sea, especially the people from Barra, Eriskay and Stornoway. The Uist ones preferred to go to the army, although quite a lot of them went to sea, but the Barraich [indigenous] headed for the sea and the girls went to mainland nursing…because there was nothing else for it, there was no other work on the island. It wasn't a choice, so I went away to sea. I got a fishing discharge from an old bodach [man] in Borve that had a wee fishing boat, and he wrote me a discharge to say I had served with him for a year or something on his fishing boat…you needed that to go away and go to the pool in Glasgow where you registered as a seaman. You produced this bit of paper…there was plenty of my type there from Barra, we were all in the same boat. I joined a ship in Liverpool and we went to Galveston, Texas to bring a load of sulphur to the UK. I was a bit sea-sick for a couple of days, but when I got over that I joined another ship. There were ten of us from Barra on that ship and there are only two of us alive today, me and Iain Sinclair up in Glen. We were away for over a year on that voyage. We went to the West Indies through the Panama Canal up to Singapore, China, Hong Kong, before going on a tramp ship – you just went from port to

A young Seonaidh Beaton

port wherever there was a cargo and you were shifted all over the place, all over the world really. So I went from China down to Australia, did all the ports there – Fremantle, Melbourne, Sydney, Adelaide, Port Elizabeth – and then down to New Zealand and brought back a cargo of coal to the UK. Coal!"

During the interview I felt like a fish hooked by Seonaidh's line of thought and wriggled helplessly with laughter when he described the importance of a good cook on board. This is what he says.

"I was on one of those tankers Eagle Oil, and some were good but this tanker was terrible, and we were away for about eight or nine months. The food was absolutely awful, and I remember there were three or four of us from Barra and we were that hungry. The cook was rubbish, he couldn't cook to save himself…[laughing]… and the officers used to get a different menu. I remember one time I was passing the galley and I saw this chicken, and to see a chicken being cooked was very rare, and the smell so good I stole the chicken…[laughing]…and I took it down to the cabin. There was a couple of us from Barra in the room so we locked the door and it was the best feed we had in ages. When it came to feeding the captain there was no chicken and the cook went mental. He didn't know where it had gone, it had taken wings and flew off. We then threw the bones out the port hole…"

Seonaidh's initiative might have satisfied his immediate hunger, but I realised during our chat that it also nourished a deep rooted desire to develop his mariner skills, or perhaps he just fancied a more discerning menu of food. This is what he says.

"I was determined I wasn't going to be an AB [able bodied seaman] all my life so I started studying and getting books and eventually I got all my certificates right up to master. I worked on the P&O ferries going to Belfast. But the Troubles started there in Ireland and they took the boats off the run, so I got a job with the Ministry of Defence and I spent the next eighteen years there. I was skipper on one of the biggest ships they had, maintaining all the moorings around the British coast and sometimes we'd do trials with the Americans. We would go out south of Iceland. During this time it was the Cold War and we used to stop on this trench, a deep trench, and we used to put this thing onto the stern of the boat. The Americans used to listen to this thing. We would stop all the engines, all the generators, all the sounds whatsoever, and they were listening to the fish because the sound of the fish is like the sound of submarines and they were trying to listen out for Russian submarines. Maybe it was Russian fish they heard...[laughing]. We spent ten days out there rolling our guts out listening to the comedians down in the box listening to the fish!"

Governments may alter the political landscape of our lives but the support, love and camaraderie of friends and family remain steadfastly our compass points as we navigate life's ocean. Those and the music and language of his island culture have always brought Seonaidh home safe and well.

Seonaidh Beaton has been working for sixty-seven years and is recovering from a knee operation.

Seonaidh with Deege Wilson

# Holiday tripper

*Interviewed on 17.08.12*

**Clare Brett**

Clare Brett likes collie dogs. She has a particular love of Barra collies. Last summer after she and her husband, Giles, and two friends had spent a wonderful afternoon lazing on Cleit beach, they stopped outside my home to admire my own delightful, barking mad Seumus. Clare is a psycho-analyst. At the same time I had just finished cycling home from Castlebay and I approached them from the road end direction, sandwiching them somewhat between the gate and my husband, who having gone out to see what was causing all the commotion, had become involved in a rather humorous discussion about a Palestinian flag he was flying, and there was heated discussion about its origin and significance. Identifying them as holiday trippers, I found out that Clare Brett is a holiday tripper with a difference.

What follows is Clare's story.

"I feel very, very blessed to have been coming to Barra ever since I can remember, every summer making the trip up to Barra from where I live in England with my family. Every summer I have been bringing my own children, but the connection goes away back well...my parents met on the island in 1946. My mother was living on the island, at Eoligarry, for a few years after the war, as a widow with my half-brother Crinan. But the story goes further back than that. The family of my mother's first husband, the Alexander family, had been coming to the island since 1910, so it really is a long connection. The Alexander family, from near the Bridge of Allan, they first came in 1910 and they built the house on the point at the northern tip of Traigh Mhor [big beach], down on the shore there in 1935. Their connection is Eva Alexander and her friend Marion Castles, who were young women before the First World War, and they were learning Gaelic in Fort William. Their Gaelic teacher said if you really want to learn Gaelic you'd better come and stay in Barra. And Mrs Joseph MacLean in Skallary, I think it is the house that is now a craft shop, and they stayed there. That was the beginning of the connection. They loved Barra and it is now into the fourth generation…"

Between meeting Clare and the interview, I had gained some local information about her family and learned that India and Eoligarry have something in common.

Clare takes up the story.

"During the war, there were very few visitors, and we have got this wonderful visitor's book. You can see year by year everyone who visited the house. After the war, the De Glens came after the war, Marion Castles married Louis De Glen so she was a De Glen, and it was often known as De Glen's house. Then my mother came. She had met and married her husband Sandy Alexander who had spent his boyhood holidays at the house, and she had met him and married him in India during the war. He was an engineer and had joined the Indian army during the war. She was there because my maternal grandparents lived and worked in India, so they married. Very tragically Sandy contracted polio and died, so my mother was left as a young widow, pregnant and expecting her first child who is my half-brother Crinan. So when she was able to come back in a convoy during the war, in very difficult conditions, her one idea was to come to Scotland and meet the Alexander relatives, and then particularly to come to Barra which she had heard so much about from Sandy. He had even taught her a few words of Gaelic, and taught her about the hills and the neighbours. When she came here she decided this was where she wanted to live with the baby. Here in Eoligarry with her child, in a house with no electricity and no running water. I think those years made such a strong connection because she felt so welcomed by the Eoligarry community. She kept her vegetables, and then my father came as a young doctor to visit through the De Glen connection. The Coddy[1] suggested he become the Barra doctor, but he was living in London. He persuaded my mum to come away and become a doctor's wife. It was a very hard decision, but she eventually agreed on the grounds that we came back every summer to the house. It is my mother's birthday, she is ninety two today, and she is determined to get up here as often as she can."

In five minutes of recording time, a very short space of time, over one hundred years had passed; a century of a family's timeline shaped by world events. I was trying to contextualise that with this remote house, cut off during the high tide. No electricity to light its windows but a fierce sense of belonging keeping the candles and the paraffin lamps burning bright.

Clare and her siblings Crinan, Richard, Maggie and Rob jostle every year allocating their trip to Barra. Clare is mother to five sons Jamie, Luke, Brendan, Daniel and Aiden who all love coming to stay in the house in Eoligarry. Clare Brett is confident her pilgrimage and connections with the island will continue forever.

---

[1] The Coddy was John MacPherson of Northbay who was nicknamed 'the Coddy' and delighted in telling the folk tales about the island and the stories that threaded the community together. He was friends with John Lorne Campbell and Compton MacKenzie of *Whisky Galore* fame. His family still stay in the same house in Northbay.

Clare Brett

Clare Brett's mother

CHAPTER THREE

# Doctor, Dentist, Nurse

Town. Sophie is in Anglesey, and Tom is in Glasgow, probably going down to England later in the year, and Megan is still at university in Manchester. I don't think any of them will be coming back to the island, but we will have to wait and see. Some years we all come together although I think it is only Tom and Megan who are coming back this year. No grandchildren yet."

Active sports have always lead to good health and Dr. Bickle with his wife Hella set up a successful club.

"I have been involved in Barra Water sports since 1983 or 1984 when we acquired some dinghies. I think the toppers were bought in 1985 which means we are going to be twenty five next year. The children here on the island have loved being involved in the water sports, and I have to say I have enjoyed dipping in and out of Castlebay on boats. I think it is very important for children who are going to spend the rest of their lives on boats, and you can't learn when you are older the same skills you can learn when you are young. Appreciating wind direction is so important. Children have to cope with the fear of capsizing and get used to the indignity of the capsize. A bit of indignity does no-one any harm. Two handed dinghies will definitely teach team building skills.

I am three years away from retiral. I would like to do thirty years which I think is long enough for anyone here on Barra. Then I hope to sail round the world, if I am fit enough. I have a boat – a catamaran – which was built in Thailand, and which is now in Portugal on its way home. Hopefully she will be arriving next year in Barra.

I want to see my children settle down, and settle back down on Barra, if I haven't found a watery grave."

Dr. Bickle now spends his life sailing the globe and was last seen sailing into the port of Antigua.

# Dentist

*Interviewed on 23.02.14*

**Robert McIntosh**

On Barra Robert McIntosh is affectionately known as *Robert the dentist.*
This is his story.

"Chatting like this is strange because you must remember I usually talk to people and they can't respond. The days of dentists telling people what they should be doing are long gone and it is very much a negotiation as to what care people want and when they want it. I am very fortunate I can work like that. I am sure both the Christines think this is a good working environment and we hope we can continue to work like that. Most people on the island know that my dental nurses are both called Christine. It makes it very easy, Christine Kojack and Christine Campbell. I couldn't do my job, or enjoy my professional life, without their continuing help and forbearance. Yep, that's the Christines. I think everyone knows them as Christine One and Christine Two.

I am not a Barraich as Christine Kojack will be shouting out. I am from England. I was born in a place called Beckenham in Kent, and am very proud that I also have a Turks and Caicos nationality that I was given after living there for eleven or twelve years. It is where I lived before coming here. Beckenham is south London now. My dad is from south London, but my mum is from Lincolnshire. My dad was a teacher and trained there and my mum trained there too, so it is where my sisters were brought up. I have very good memories of it.

My first dental memory is of an old dentist in Newcastle-Upon-Tyne who removed four of my first teeth, my premolars, with the aid of nitro oxide. It is an indelible memory for me. I remember my dad took me home and I told him I felt great which was my first attempt at sarcasm.

The way I got into dentistry was later in life when I was in my final years at school. My best friend's father was a dentist and I can remember being very, very impressed by the individual, John Greenwood. He had a seemingly very, very interesting and rewarding life, and that was really the inspiration for me to do dentistry.

John Greenwood was very kind over the years in that he nurtured my interest and persuaded me to go and train at the University of Leeds where he had been a graduate. I was very saddened to hear news of his death a couple of years ago. It came at a time when I was doing an MSc at Glasgow University, and I was able to dedicate the thesis to John Greenwood. I am very glad I could do that because I am sure he would have been very proud of my progression in dentistry.

So that's how I got involved in dentistry. It is like giving something back. I remember being at John Greenwood's funeral and I was with a neighbour of John and Pat's, Robin who had gone on to do dentistry. John had three sons and none of them had wanted to go on and do dentistry. I hadn't quite realised how closely he had followed both of our careers in the way that he had done. I remember after the funeral chatting to Pat and she said, 'Well, you know, you and Robin were just like two extra boys in the family'. I owe an awful lot to John Greenwood and his dentistry, and also his son who was my best friend at school. I used to sail dinghies with him. I was always interested in sailing. Young John was a very good sailor, and we made a good team together. He was a very good technical sailor, and we did a lot of racing and things like that. We sailed for Nottingham and Derbyshire in the schoolboy championships, and we went on to national championships in our senior years. I thoroughly enjoyed that."

Robert has always had a desire to serve people and his country.

"I qualified in December of 1982, and I was actually fortunate to be awarded a cadetship in my final year of dentistry which was great. They paid me to do my studying which meant I had more money to spend. I joined the army on the fourth of January 1982, and, much to my mother's anguish, the Falklands came up in the spring of that year. I remember writing a letter to the head of dental services volunteering my services as a dental student to go to Aldershot. Fortunately for the people of Aldershot, my services weren't required. I finished my dental course then I was signed up to serve in the army on a short term commission of five years. My first posting was working in the army hospital down in Woolwich, in the oral surgery department, which was very good and built up my confidence in oral surgery. There is a very good saying in dentistry that you have to be able to take teeth out or apply the healing tongs. So I gained more experience in oral surgery. After about six weeks I went off to Sandhurst where I was trained in the ways of being an officer and a gentleman, and played the best games of *Cowboys and Indians* over the fields at Sandhurst. My first posting was to Harrogate, the wilds of West Yorkshire, literally twelve miles away from where I had lived for the previous five years.

That was how I started in the army. It was a great experience. In the days when I started you had your qualification and then you went straight out into the busy world of general practice, with the financial burdens of having to carry out the business of dentistry. Whereas working in the army, I think, allowed me to develop my skills without any financial pressures which I think was very, very good. So I served five years in the army, and decided after four years I didn't really want it to become my full career.

I was fortunate then to spend the last two years of my time in south Germany on the Rhine. It gave me a taste for things continental and things European. There is an old army saying, you make a lot of acquaintances but maybe not a lot of friends. Generally most postings in the army at that time were for three years, so you could probably reckon to get to know someone for a period of about eighteen months or so. I did make a few friends in the army, but sadly I have lost touch, because in those days the army was being reduced. It was the days of Margaret Thatcher, and it was about making the army more efficient; equipping the fighting forces rather than a heavy financial commitment to the support services. So a lot of the dental postings were towards field units, and dentists would go with the field unit hospitals. A lot of the training unit establishments were removed."

MacIntosh, of course, is a Scottish name, and I wondered if Robert had come to find his roots – no pun intended!

Robert McIntosh

"I had the distinction of being the last dentist to have served at the Bridge of Don in Aberdeen which was the Scottish Infantry Depot junior soldiers training establishment. It was the first time I came to Scotland and I found that I actually quite liked it. However a job became available in the Turks and Caicos and subsequently I worked there. I was the only dentist on the island and it was a developing country, and I enjoyed it. Life in the Turks and Caicos was at a great time when a lot of development work was just starting. The people were wonderful and really appreciated the skills I brought to the island.

I was working in a medical building with a guy who subsequently became a great friend – Ewan Menzies. Both our practices expanded during the next twelve years. Again I was happy. It is so nice always being warm. I really liked that aspect of it. I sometimes reflect and have fond memories of Caribbean evenings, flip flops, Hawaiian shirts, shorts and a Green Becks listening to the Turks and Caicos version of *Red Red Wine.*

I remember the world got more muddled after an evening dancing. Ewan and I became involved in politics on the island and subsequently stood for election. We didn't get elected but readily appreciated that our contributions in the political field weren't as welcome as our contributions in the professional field. Our interests diverged after that. Of course, by this time I was married, and the long term plans for Jamie, my son, needed careful consideration. That's when I met Christine MacMillan from Stornoway who was the former cardio when I had been in the army on a temporary posting in Benbecula. We had met at a London summer school where I was studying for an MSc, and Christine had told me about a job in Barra."

Certain names signpost people's lives and another Christine brought him to Barra.

"I love what I am doing here on Barra. I came with my wife and son, and I started working here in 1998. It has been a while.

I graduated with an MSc in primary dental care with a specialism in orthodontics and it is what I enjoy doing. I am responsible for providing the orthodontic service for the southerly isles here. I travel about quite a bit and I liked my course. I think it is important to keep your skills up to date. I am required to be away from Barra. The gentleman who supervised my training was Professor Jim MacDonald whose mother came from Barra. I met Jim in the surgery in Barra and I didn't know he was a professor of orthodontics. He came and asked me for a favour, but I didn't conduct as rigorous an examination of his problem as I should have, but we just smiled about it and it has formed the basis of an ongoing friendship.

Jim has a place up in Eoligarry, and he visits every so often. Jim supervised the orthodontic part of the practice in Glasgow and was very kind in offering me a clinical assistantship within his department over in Kirkcaldy. The organisation NESS, who sponsored my MSc and sponsored my travelling with Prof MacDonald over in Kirkcaldy, have been very good to me. It has greatly enhanced my orthodontic skills and my diagnostic skills which are so important when you are a long way away from the specialist centres in Glasgow. I have been very grateful for the support I have had from the consultants in the dental hospital, particularly Douglas Forsyth, and more latterly Alastair Gardner who indulged me with my diagnostic reasoning for formulating treatment plans which I was then able to carry out.

In Islay the orthodontic service are asking questions as to whether the people in Islay are actually having equitable access to the service. Patients are flown from Islay to Glasgow to have their treatment done, but not all of the patients who require treatment can be accommodated within that service design. So here in the islands, in the rural and remote places, it is imperative that people have the most equitable access to the treatment service available, and that requires more experienced practitioners taking on a bigger degree of responsibility, but also being alive to the limitations within their own practices and being alive to the services that are readily available.

I am a volunteer of the Coastguard, and I enjoy it. It is a good team, and having a bit more time than most others I have assumed the responsibility of Station Officer. I like the work. We go out and about and make sure that hospital patients can be taken off the island in an emergency.

Island life just is… I foresee staying on Barra. I hope that doesn't disappoint either of the two Christines too much, but I like being able to go about the islands, and continue doing orthodontic treatment on the mainland. I would like to thank the island community for putting up with me for fifteen years, and I do plan to stay."

There is a ring of confidence around Barra because *Robert the dentist* is simply the best dentist in the whole world.

# Nurse

*Interviewed on 09.02.12*

**M**airi a' Welder, Mairi MacKinnon's father was a welder and forged her and all her siblings so well they are all known by his profession. This is her story.

"On Barra I am known as Mairi a' Welder because I think my father had a welding plant when he came back to Barra to live and it was easier than calling us anything else because there were so many other MacKinnons. It was a nickname. My brothers are called Doo-da a' Welder, Murdo a' Welder and Donald a' Welder. That's how we are listed in the Barra Phoney[1].

I think nicknames are very significant especially when there are so many MacKinnons and so many MacNeils. Probably the only way to differentiate them was to give them a nickname. You find it in Uist, but I think Barra has more nicknames than the other islands have.

I live in Nasg on the road to Vatersay, at the end of the Nasg road just before you head up to the monument. It was a croft we got after we came to Barra. A friend of mine who was leaving the island, she gave it to us, and we built our own house. But it is becoming more difficult to get a croft. A lot of the young ones are wanting crofts to build on.

I am a Barraich. I was born on Barra, but my parents lived in Glasgow for a few years before coming back to Barra, and two of my brothers were born there. And, of course, when I was away at

---

[1] Barra Phoney is the local phone book of the island which is published by Voluntary Action Barra and Vatersay. It includes all the residents of the island and their nickname. When you live on Barra many people are known by their nicknames purely to distinguish one Dòmhnall MacNeil from the other Dòmhnall MacNeil. It is not unusual to find such listings as 'Eppa' – Mairi Mhol's daughter.

school I wasn't on the island.

We had to go to Inverness; it was before regionalisation and had to go to the Academy there in the county of Inverness. Well, we did the first three years in Castlebay, and then we went on to Inverness. At that time it took ten hours for the ferry to get here, so we stayed for a term and only came home at Christmas and Easter. It was very hard.

There was quite a few of us. It wasn't nice. The food was poor and we were quite restricted. We had to get up and go to mass in the morning and do housework on a Saturday. It was quite regimental. After that I just came back for a short period of time and worked in one of the shops here until I was seventeen and a half, and I left to join nursing."

Mairi did not follow her father's footsteps into the welding trade.

"All my life really I have been a nurse. I did my training, then my midwifery, then my district. I was in Glasgow for a while, and then Dunoon, and then got married and came back home. I worked in the district here, and then at St. Brendan's for twenty one years.

I do think nursing today is different but I wouldn't like to say there has been a decline, it is just there has been so much new technology from when we were doing our training. Everything has advanced so much. I still think the matrons should be back because when they changed onto the Salmon thing…[2] and there have been a few other changes since then. I have lost touch with all the rest of it. I think in the days of the matron

---

[2] The Salmon Committee was set up in 1968 to generate a senior career structure for nurses. However Lord Salmon disparaged nursing and prescribed the Nursing Officer roles to be divorced from any clinical engagement. Some nurses received higher pay scales but the agreement did nothing to enhance the profession's standing or influence. Ultimately it diminished the value of working in the clinical situation.

there was the one chief and then people coming down after her. I think it was better then

I think it is still the same as it was in my day, that some of the nurses had a lot of patience and some of them didn't, but I think the nurses have more reports to write and I don't think the computer helps. Nurses are doing more like taking bloods and if you have a good nurse, with a good bedside manner, they still have the time for the patient.

Cleanliness, especially in the hospitals on the mainland, is not as it should be and that's because of all these contracts. The maids have been done away with. They were employed by the NHS and each ward had its own maid under the sister. They were very proud of their wards, whereas putting it out to tender anyone is coming in and out. It is a business, and that's it. They are not employed by the NHS, so there is not the same interest in it, is there?

I just enjoyed nursing at St. Brendan's. Every day was a pleasure. I started in St. Brendan's when it opened twenty years ago. That was the home, and it had twenty residential beds and five hospital beds – two long term and three emergency beds run by the NHS, and the home was run by the council.

It is still the same but there have been changes in residential care so everyone has an en suite. Hopefully there will be a new hospital soon."

Buildings change on Barra just like the roads, and Mairi describes improvements and life before them.

"There have been some changes since I came back, the two causeways – one to Vatersay and the one to Eriskay. I did relief in Vatersay and had to go over on the small boat in the morning and then back over later on. There was an old car that was left there, the National Health Service left it so that it could be used. It took ten to fifteen minutes, but you didn't go if it was too rough. There was a nurse there who attended to the needs of the Vatersay community. She was part-time.

On Vatersay they were able to come and go whenever they liked. Sad that they have lost the school now, and that they are not so self-contained. They are more part of Barra but I don't think they would like to hear that because they like their own identity.

The Uist causeways mean you can almost go to Stornoway in one day, and the services can come over."

When not nursing the community, Mairi scripts many a play for the island's drama group.

"I was asked by Mairi Jean, and I just joined them. Mairi has stopped now. I just got involved to do it locally for a laugh. That's what makes it so enjoyable, because everyone comes out for a drama. The last one was about the big house in Eoligarry and, after having the exhibition at the Heritage about the raids in Eoligarry, we thought it would be good to do some research on it and produce a drama.

Mairi a' Welder

The play gave the side of the MacGillivrays living there. They didn't treat the people very well at all, and that was the truth of it. It was very hard for them, the island people. So after WW1 the people just rose up and demanded some land.

I didn't write it. It was Mary Ceit MacKinnon who wrote it, with a wee bit of help from some of us because Mary Ceit and Mary Catherine had gone, before the exhibition opened, to the archives in Edinburgh to get information because we really didn't have much, not nearly as much as we had about the Vatersay raiders for the Mingulay exhibition. So they went to get background material, so it was very authentic.

The costumes are whatever is in the box, whatever people can find. I had two roles in it because Annag who does these parts, she was Kirsty from Tiree, and I was someone's wife at the end. You just sort of think of people in the community for certain parts, and it is great when they say yes. It is really hard to get people together sometimes. There were sixteen people and I think we only had two rehearsals.

Sometimes it depends what is happening on the island whether we put something on or not. Last year it was a MacNeil gathering and we did a sketch then, but there are no plans at the moment. We sometimes don't do anything until a couple of weeks beforehand. I know it is the centenary of Mingulay this year, and I know we will be putting something on, and hopefully a visit to Mingulay.

I am active in the Heritage Committee and the Heritage Centre because it promotes the culture of the island and the language and that sort of thing. There are lots of old photographs, old school records that can be checked up on, and there is a small café attached to it. It is the history of the island and all the different happenings going way, way back. A lot of people come to see their mother's home.

We have one part-time person who runs it and nine volunteers – it is run mostly by volunteers. We celebrate St. Bride on the first of February, or Michaelmas, or something like that, just a wee ceilidh. It is a nice and comfortable cosy venue, everyone together."

Mairi's proud of her heritage and encourages the use of Gaelic. This is what she says.

"Gaelic is very important. Well, it was our first language and it is much more expressive. You can express yourself much better in our language than in English.

Well, we feel that anyway. I think there are a lot more adjectives in Gaelic than there are in English. Say, for example, beautiful. Well, there is *snog* and *breagha* – these sort of words. And of course all our culture is based on the Gaelic language as well, so I find it very important. I hope it is not going to die out the way it seems to be.

Well, it is very important. I think it might not be dying. But we were always too polite, and we always spoke in English if a non-Gaelic speaker was there, but now we continue to speak in Gaelic. You see, we were taught in English but before my generation I think they were discouraged to speak it. Drama, I think, helps the young ones to understand the language. Whereas singing, you can learn it parrot fashion, but with the drama you need to understand it and interact with it. I think it would help if we had a young person's Gaelic drama group on the island."

CHAPTER FOUR

# Barra's Burly Boys

## Fisherman, Wandering Star & Drummer

# Fisherman

*Interviewed on 01.03.10*

Willie Douglas

Willie Douglas is a fisherman, a pier operative, a fire fighter and a community activist. One of seven children he and his siblings are affectionately known as *the crows,* although by the time I interviewed Willie he had gone grey. Living in Barra all his life he can trace his family back to the year dot. He lives on the east side in Skallary. When I first met Willie he was working in the local co-operative store. He told me there were many chapters in his book.

This is his story,

"My heritage in Barra is MacIntyre from time immemorial, but I have also got Oban and Mull and a lot of Uist in me – although I don't like to publicise that… [laughter]. I was actually born in Uist, by mistake [laughter]. There are plenty of chapters in my book. I have always been the kind of person who loves variety in life. Variety is the spice of life they say.

I have basically been a fisherman at heart. I wanted to be a fisherman before I went to primary school. I wanted to go to sea and join the Merchant Navy, and I wanted to get married. I used to tell the old women I would go to visit – they would quiz and question you, I would tell them my plans then and they were amazed that just a wee tot could go around with all these plans. I have fulfilled most of them.

I work for the Western Isles Council as pier operative in Barra. I look after the piers and make sure they are in a tidy and clean condition and generally supervise any large vessel coming in and out. The oil tanker comes in once a month, so I just make sure everything is tickety-boo for her and any help I can give the fishermen with their daily toils. You just help and look after them.

Well, over the years I have done quite a lot. I have my Under 16.5 metre Fishing Ticket. I have got my Grade One Boat Masters, AB from the Merchant Navy, and generally all from the marine industry and all its facets. There are quite a lot of courses and it takes a long time to gather all these skills together. If you have got that kind of background, obviously you are going to be skipper of a concrete pier! People who are going to be in charge of things, they like them to know what they are going to be doing. So, yeah, there is quite a lot of knowledge and background to it, because if things go wrong you have got to know where to go and what to do."

Willie is also watch manager for the Highlands and Islands Fire Service. He visits homes and suggests fire prevention initiatives as well as actively involving the young people of the community. This is what he says.

"I have just celebrated passing my twenty year service. I am Watch Manager OIC, the officer in charge of Castlebay fire

station. I succeeded from Donald MacIlvan last Christmas there, and I had great training from him in how to be a boss [laughter]. I am a better fire-fighter, but he is a good boss to work for via the job. We do a lot of fire prevention. The biggest cause of fires on the island is cigarettes – stop smoking – and in the kitchen, chip pans, old fashioned chip pans. Throw it out, get a thermostatically controlled deep fryer. It is a wee bit of common sense, use your common sense. On Barra and Vatersay people do use their common sense, but we don't only deal with fires. If you fall in a loch or burn, it is us who will be coming out to help you. If you stick your toe in the tap, it will be some big burly boys coming in to rescue you."

Conversation with Willie was so filled with enthusiasm, I began planning to deliberately stick my toe where it shouldn't go to luxuriate in the warm safety of Barra's 'big, burly boys'!

Passionate, Willie believes island living is all about opportunities.

This is what he says.

"You do as many things as you can, and do them as well as you can. I think we are very, very fortunate on the islands that we can do lots of things, whereas on the mainland you are pigeon-holed into something and the opportunities don't arise. It is more full-time, but here on the islands there are more opportunities. You have part-time work. I have been on the lifeboat, I have been on the coastguard, I have worked on the ambulance for a very short time, in fact the only blue light I haven't worked under is the police. These opportunities don't arise on the mainland and it is fantastic that you can do it here.

I am involved with the Northbay Port Users, which is the users group for the Northbay Harbour area and it includes Ardveenish. It is made up of fishermen and anybody that has basically got a boat, so that is pleasure then leisure and commercials that run out of Northbay. I am chairman of that, a co-founder along with Ian Dewar and a couple of others. That has really benefited the area down there. Prior to that there was no voice as such, and the powers-that-be don't like listening to just one voice complaining, so I realised that and helped form the Northbay users so that we could have a coherent voice.

I am also involved with the Barra and Vatersay Company Limited to try to develop the island's potential and to develop the island culturally, financially and in every sense of the word because we have got to do it, no one else will. The way the financial climate is, we should be able to do more for ourselves and have more control. Empowerment in the community, for the community to help themselves, rather than going with a bowl to the Highlands and Islands Enterprise, or the Scottish Government, or European Union, constantly looking for cash to do this, that and the next thing. If we can generate funding for ourselves…there is a fantastic wealth of talent on this island. People just don't realise the amount of talented people there are. Sometimes I feel as if I am out of my depth in the room with these people, and of course the company is owned by the people on the island. We have a very strong membership compared to other communities in the Highlands and Islands, so it is representative of the community. For nothing to happen all you have to do is sit at home, and nothing will happen. But if you do just a little bit, and everyone did the same, then it's amazing how much can get done."

Variety is definitely the spice of Willie Douglas's life. If he did not live on Barra I could see him simultaneously running campaigns for various groups like a clever juggler keeping so many balls in the air. Willie believes Barra is the best place on earth and after an hour in his company I couldn't disagree.

# The Wandering Star

*Interviewed on 18.07.13*

**Calum MacNeil**

On a hot July afternoon in 2013 I found Uilliem-the
-butcher laughing with a rather animated gentleman
behind the fruit counter. Excitedly he ushered me over,
introducing me to one of the funniest men I think I have ever
had the pleasure to know.

Before leaving Barra at the ripe old age of sixteen and half,
Calum MacNeil son of the Rionnag from Eoligarry, used to hang
dead rabbits from his windowsill to sell to passing trade. His
story is the journey of a shooting star. This is what he says.

"I have always stopped in Barra. I am from Eoligarry and I went
to Castlebay University! I stayed in Nasg during the week. I always
remember putting a pair of rabbits across my fence outside my
room, and everyone who went to school with me would know
that, and that shows you how much education I had. It was the
rabbits that were important, and at midday I would go down to
Horve and sell them. I went to school with Ruraidh Pheiter. I am
going to dinner with him tomorrow night.

I left Barra when I was sixteen and a half, with my uncle
Ruiraidh a' Phosta, who was a character on his own, and
Dhomhnaill Mac a' Phosta my other first cousin. We have a
picture in the Heritage Centre [Dualchas] of him. I arrived in
Glasgow, and talk about refugees! Mairi a' Diac gave me a coat,
Iain a' Noon gave me the pants, and when my mate in Stornoway
first seen us he laughed non-stop. There was no thrift shop then,
it was just hand-me-downs. Relations who were skippers and
mates and my mother thought they would have a bit of clothes
for me because Ruraidh gave his nephew a coat and so they took
us to Glasgow.

Of course we had the famous fishing discharges signed by the

Coddy or by a priest. That was very important. I can't mind who signed mine. I didn't care. It was my fishing discharge, and some don't remember, but it was about your navigational skills and we could sail anywhere in the world. So people just went to sea. We were so ahead of city people that when we went to Glasgow we had two years under our belts as fishermen, and that gave us our EDH [Efficient Deck Hand], or an SOS [Senior Ordinary

Calum MacNeil

Seaman] which put you two notches above the poor bugger that was born and brought up in Glasgow. That was how the big ball bounced in those days. I was on the watch with a guy from Glasgow, *Nanna* or something. Oh, when he first started talking, he had no teeth to start with and I couldn't understand the Glasgow slang, I was completely bamboozled…and all the buses and the electricity –don't forget we had no running water and the bucket.

In fact, talking about buckets. Eoghanna a' Bhailidh, who is now living in Castlebay, and I got paid off a key boat and I had the biggest pay off – £108. This is going back a long time. I came back to Eoligarry and my mother, thinking about the rabbits, got me up early in the morning to carry two empty buckets of water. After being round the world for a year and half, here I am with a hundred odd pounds in my pocket, and I can't get anyone to carry the water for me. And I thought, 'Hey Calum, it is time to move on'. I gave it deep thought. All that money and no one would carry a bucket of water for you. It was all pride. So we would get on the boats at Uist and go to Oban and then get the train to Glasgow. We all had long lives and some did very, very well I must say."

Like Hesperus, Calum's world was illuminated by antipodean adventures opening his eyes to the sparkling rays of different cultures.

"In the beginning I was in the Merchant Navy. I did a total of about three years, long enough to achieve EDH. When I was on a star boat to Australia I asked about to see how far an EDH would take me, and I was told it stands as good as an AB [Able Bodied Seaman] in Australia. So bye bye star boat, and Calum Mary comes ashore in Australia. Allen [Mhols, the blacksmiths] – they had loads of money, we had nothing, absolutely zilch, so anyway he had a new suitcase and I thought if I go ashore with a bag they will surely pick me up. So I stole Allan Mhol's suitcase and took a lifeboat ashore, that's a long story I won't go into that, but ended up ashore in Sydney. Cook a' Chlachair, another Barra fellow, came with me to live in a doss house for a couple of weeks and got a job. Goodness me, when I think of the concentration camps! Our first job in Australia was bones in a slaughter house. They would put them in a mixing bowl and mix them and then take the tallow out of them. Our job was to empty it. I thought about leaving Barra and that I didn't like this job either. I quietly made my way down to the waterfront and I got a job on the waterfront.

Beautiful job, beautiful money, beautiful everything. I took Cook a' Chlachair with me and we stayed with a Jewish family, and, my God, when I think of it she was good to us. She knew that we were refugees because she was a refugee herself. She gave us soup and everything. We didn't know how to cook. In Eoligarry you boiled a rabbit and ate it, so you had a cockerel and everything was in soup and boiled and you ate it. No grease, no fat, no nothing. You ate, and that's what happened there.

On the waterfront we ended up in a Maltese gang. I don't mean *gang*, they work in gangs on ships. The Australians thought I was a *diego* because my English was very, very poor, so they sent us with the Maltese and they were great. But we had a hard time in the city because when we went for a beer we were called *you diego son-of-a-gun*. So the Maltese gang took us to their club and we sat in their club yapping away in our language and they would yap in theirs, and we had a great time telling stories. On the water front you would meet a lot of really good people from Barra. I never spoke English, just Gaelic. I was just a longshoreman. My wages went from about £13 a month to nine shillings an hour plus time and half. I was throwing money around like a paper hanger. I couldn't hold onto it because it was so plentiful. We had a great time with it."

A burning flame is restless and Calum soon found himself reaching for the dizzy heights in America.

Here's what happened.

"I was deported back to Barra. I used to flog a lot of Fuji transistor radios for the '*chinaman*' and all the boys know that. Well because I sold so much for him he gave me a little gift, a tartan bag, and I jumped ship in Boston. Actually I was painting the bridge in Boston when they came after me and caught me. I asked the immigration officials how did they know it was me. My landlady told the officials that I would be carrying a tartan bag! In the meantime in Boston everyone is crying, not wanting to be deported, but I got a typewriter and sent a letter to Iain in Queensland and the guys sent me twenty or thirty dollars which was a lot of money then. They took me to the airport and they walked me up to my seat and the pilot took my passport. I felt like a real heel as if I was going to jump off the plane.

In London with the money they gave me, I bought cigars at the airport thinking I could flog them in London, but that didn't go too well. I had no clothes and I was this huge man. I was sent to London. I had heard of the Mason Hotel from the boys. The bus took me to the middle of London and I knew the hotel but before I got there I knew there was a mission. So I knocked at the door, and I will never forget, some faces you always remember. It was really cold and damp, and this little guy about fifty-five opened the door to me. I asked do you have any clothes I could wear? Anyway, he went to a morgue or something and he gave me a big coat that would fit me.

I then met the guys who were working on the canal [Panama] and half of them I knew from Auckland and Sydney, I went to school with them. They were spending the last of their pound notes, and I was drinking it as fast as they were spending it. So I asked them where they were staying, and they told me about this Catholic mission, a brand new one. I went up and I was the best Catholic in the world by then. They told me where to go to the office, and I gave them the hardest luck story, that I was helping people out and got the socialist bit in and that. And of course

Calum MacNeil

got sympathy and all that. Well the seamen were all sharing two to a room, but I went upstairs and got a room with a big bath and shower all to myself. I told the mission my money was due to arrive in seven days, and he believed me. But like in the biblical story, on the seventh day Calum disappeared into the ether, because my mother sent me money to get home to Barra!

There was only one thing I didn't have, a jacket. All I had was this coat and it stunk, so I went to the pub where they were spending the money, and I got a jacket from the publican who was serving the Barra men. I was trying them all on to see what one fitted me and they were all laughing. The third jacket fitted me well and I promised to send it back. Some years later I still had the jacket the London publican had given me. I was sitting in the Waldorf Hotel in Vancouver, and this day a guy tapped me on the shoulder and he said, 'Do you remember me? I was in the pub in London.' Well, I gave him back the jacket and we had a few drinks over it!

Well, once here on Barra I got a good job as a pipefitter in the Kincardine Bridge, and I tried to get a few Barra men to work with me, but they didn't because they didn't have a certificate. I told them, 'Don't worry, I will make you one!' I stayed working there. I got money every eight weeks and I spent it in Glasgow before I went to Canada. If you had been in Barra, and controlled the way I was, then once you pass Muldonach you have a tremendous sense of freedom, and that freedom and understanding life has guided me all my life. I did the whole progressive party thing.

I headed off to Canada. My brother-in-law's brother had

a farewell party for me in a gambling joint in Glasgow. I was leaving as an engineer, but I lost all my money. I worked on the Clyde ferries for a few weeks to get my fare to Montreal. There I was a complete stranger, and they put me on the wrong bus. I was headed for the Catholic Mission there. In fact I was trying to get to Vietnam, but I couldn't get there from the American side and I had to go to Tokyo. I was in Montreal working in the mission toilets for the nuns, asking them what time mass was and how often. I got a job, 98 cents an hour. I had just got deported from my job in Boston at $5.95 an hour. I was in the mud. I slept on the floor because I was on nightshift, and ate the scraps that the seamen had left. I did that for a couple of weeks, then I started going down to the SIU, the union and that.

I got a call saying, 'Right Scotty, can you start?' I did about six to nine months on the lakes, then I headed to Vancouver. I got a job in a factory with Babcock and Wilcox. I didn't have a clue what I was doing. This time I was a boiler maker, and if you are Scottish or British they think you are really good at what you do. As luck would have it, they were training the top apprentice of the province of British Columbia. I was asked to train him and told him a good few stories, then told him you better get on with it if you are learning the job, so he did. We were making the tugs for the Bayell Straits. Half were made in the factory and the other sent by truck. It was all Greek to me, but all the guys were as pleased as punch because I was telling them all good stories. I didn't know it but the apprentice was going to the boss and saying what a great tradesman I was. I found that out because I told him I was leaving.

Then I went to the shipyards, having served my time on the Barra shipyards, and again I had good references from there. I had no tools except what I bought from a pawn shop, but I lost them after the bottom fell out of the brown paper bag. This big foreman from Greenock, a real stickler, asked me where my tools were, and I told him they were being sent on. He asked me about the Barra shipyards, and I told him I worked on making the shaft for the Queen Mary! He never asked me another question after that.

From there I met Norman MacKenzie who was an engineer and I got him a job. There was a leak on the shaft on one of the ships used to push the logs and the lumber, and this boat kept sinking. I supposedly patched it up, and the guys were saying don't worry Scotty has fixed it. Well, talk about scared! It was empty going up, but when the logs were on it the boat sunk everything. Obviously I didn't put the grind in but I didn't know what I did wrong, but word came round the shipyards and the boss came down and asked what I had done. I told him I thought I had fixed it. Then I knew it was time to move on.

Me and my buddy Norman headed up to Alaska, to a copper mine where it was heavy-duty mechanics. So with my experience in Barra... We had to go underground for eleven miles to get to the mine, and then the mine was up on the outside, but Norman was good. I remember the first night the snowflakes were about an inch thick and they floated down. All the workers were Polish and I used to lock myself in the explosive boxes to hide unless there was an explosion. My friend, Iain from Stornoway, had a very bad accident there and lost his life. That put me off mining forever.

I brought his body home [to the Isle of Lewis]. I was the only person in Vancouver who knew his mother and father, so that's why I have always gone to Lewis. It was tough. The company, based in New York, did not notify the family and his father had been a police chief in London. I was thousands of miles away, and it was me who had to phone him. It was terrible.

It was a Lewis man who owned a hotel there and found out I was from Barra, and heard about Iain, and took us in. Chrissie Wilson, who is from Vancouver, she found out about it and she paid for all the phone calls. When we returned to Vancouver they had collected $2000 dollars for him. One of the people there that I still keep in contact with put $500 into the collection. Fantastic people there.

I used to sell perfume from Barra at all the different Highland Games in Canada. I used to tell everyone how big the factory was and I even convinced myself how big it was. Tourists used to say

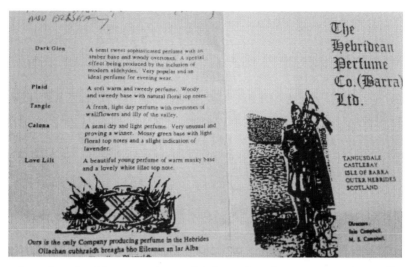

when they had been to Barra, 'Calum that factory must be really small,' and I would tell them they had been to the wrong side of Barra.

The perfume came by mail order from Barra. It was oil extracted from the flowers of the machair and there was a pile of people on the island squishing the flowers. You couldn't believe what people would tell you. I always sold out of it. It was all Non's perfume[1] and they were putting the oil in the bottle by a syringe and I was telling people of this huge factory...small stores were distributing it along with the heather. Scott McAulay, the piper, his father took these two young guys from Toronto and they were at the Games up in Hamilton. They saw Hebridean perfume and asked where it was from, along with the heather, and listened to the spiel I gave them.

It was a Yugoslav who planted the heather in North Carolina for button holes and I bought some and sold it *from Barra*. I told them that on a Saturday afternoon in Barra we pick up a couple

---

[1] 'Non', John Campbell lives in a croft house in Tangusdale. He is a taxi driver on the island. From 1969 to the mid seventies Non and Robert Armstrong sold a range of beauty products made on Barra the length and breadth of Scotland. This was produced in a small room in the croft of Non's mother. Non is a nickname which came from his uncle in Canada who died aged twenty two.

of labourers from Lewis, because they don't work on a Sunday up there, and they come to Barra and pick the heather for two days and then we ship them back to Lewis. He believed every word I told him!

I got my licence to work in Real Estate and the rest is history. I spend the winter in Florida... It is hard! I have done very well, very well indeed. I am seventy- eight and still working. I don't do anything at all, maybe one phone call every two weeks, that's all.

I am married and have two kids and they are both in Vancouver. They have been in Barra a few times. Jim McGee built me a beautiful lovely house in Eoligarry, and the MacGillivrays from Uist furnished it with beautiful quality furnishings, really superb. Jim and his wife made the beds for us.

Tha na daoine sa Bharraigh 'sa Bhatarsaigh a' deanamh uabhasach math airson iad fhin agus than a taighean uabahsach math, spaideil. Tha a h-uile sgath a than a clann g ionnsachadh cho math. Tha iad uabhasach fòrtanach agus than a foghlam aig Sgoil Bhagh a' Caisteal direach nas math na fear ann am Baile Mòr. Tha na clan ag ionnsachadh tòrr agus tha aimsir snamh anns an sgoil far a bheil a clan. ag ionnsachadh. Clann òga fuireach air an Eilean agus ionnsachadh stuth. Faodaidh dhu a' deanamh sgath sa Bharraigh. Ma tha croit agus taigh agad bi thu math. Tapa Leibh agus chi mise sibhse air bòrd bata.

The people of Barra and Vatersay are doing very well for themselves and the houses are very good and smart. Everything the children are learning is very good. They are very lucky and the education at Castlebay School is just as good as one in the big cities. The children are learning a lot and there is a swimming pool in the school where the children learn. Young children stay on the island and learn things. You can do anything in Barra. If you have a croft and a house you will be fine. Thank you and I will see you all on a boat."

Calum MacNeil, son of the Rionnag of Eoligarry, a twinkling star burning bright.

# *Drummer*

*Interviewed on 02.11.13*

**Donnie MacNeil**

Donnie MacNeil of Nasg is as much a part of Barra as the beautiful flowering machair. Wearing a uniform of protective blue overalls, black council work shoes and a skip cap, he travels the highways and byways of the island three times a week in a big dust cart, smiling and emptying the bins. Come the weekends, all polished and clean, he lifts his drumsticks and beats out the rhythms of island life as Donnie the delicious, drummer of The Vatersay Boys.

This is his story.

"I empty the bins on Barra. I love my job, it is fantastic. It is amazing the inspiration I get from the hills and the streams and the beauty of the island. I go round it three times a week. I visit every nook and cranny and I know every single house and every commercial building. Sometimes you are like a counsellor and you can be the only person to speak to some folk week on week. People think when you are on an island that you see everybody all the time. It is not like that. One time when I was in Moscow, visiting my son in the high flats, I looked out when the bins were being emptied, and one guy was emptying all the rubbish from twelve hundred people, that's like emptying Barra in one go. It was surreal. I see things when I visit different countries because I always check out what the bin men are doing. One time I was emptying a bin in Glen and I picked up this white plastic bag that had fallen out the bin and there was about fifty thousand pounds in used ten pound notes. I am only kidding you on!

I am a Barraich. I was born in Glasgow in an attic flat in Paisley Road West, home of the Uist and Barra people. My dad is from Nasg and my mum is from South Uist and I live in my father's home. I feel great living there and it feels as if this is where I should be. I have a great sense of belonging. It is fantastic. I got married when I was twenty one to a Barra girl. When I was about twenty my dad got the croft and he gave it to me but I didn't do anything with it until the time was right. No one believed that I would make the move to Barra. I decided to opt into island life. You have to make a contribution. I thought I would come up and do a bit of crofting and candle making. I have three brothers and three sisters, and he gave **me** the croft, but it didn't create any tensions. The croft, however, became like a rope round my neck because I keep getting letters from the crofting commission asking me things, and it becomes a responsibility. It was asking when I was going to work the croft.

I came to Barra seventeen years ago. My father left Barra when he was fourteen, so I have been on Barra longer than my dad stayed here. I saw life on Barra as creating something for future generations. When you are a Barra MacNeil it is a stamp on your forehead. I first came to Barra when I was three years of age, and I stayed in the house I am staying in now for about six weeks, and years after that we used to go to Garrymonie where my mother's people are from. I went to school in Glasgow, to St. Robert's Primary and St. Robert's Bellarmine. I got music in school, it was quite well known for music, and Duncan Johnstone and his brother, both really good musicians, they went there too."

When asked about music running through families, this is what he said.

"I have been playing drums since I was twelve. Drumming is not a traditional instrument, and I went to Duncan Johnstone's dad to be taught pipes, and my brother Mick went to Jim Blair School to learn the accordion. They weren't blending, and I asked my mum if I could change to drums so that I could follow Mick. My three sisters sing, and Janette was good on the piano. My sisters all sing in the Govan choir, they have just won the Mod. My dad died about two years ago. My dad played the pipes and he was a really good singer but he never really sang at concerts or anything and my mum is a good singer. My theory is that music keeps you out of trouble especially in Glasgow. It stops you from spraying your name on walls and stuff like that. Anyone who is learning an instrument has another focus. My whole family was musical and we all just had music. I didn't come to the island thinking I would get a band together. I came up to the island to live on my dad's croft. Gary Blair and I played together on ferries and I told him I was going to Barra. My crofting life didn't come about. After about six months Nollie [MacKinnon], the guitarist approached me and asked me to play. I went to rehearsal with them and big Calum MacLeod, then after that I brought my drum kit up from Glasgow.

The first song I ever wrote was over in Nasg and it is about an Australian who came from Australia to live in a council house in Northbay. It is called *The Land of My Birth*. He has now gone back to Australia. I just remember my dad used to say when he had a wee drink in him, he would say, 'My home, my home,' and I used to say, 'You are home,' but he was talking about Barra. He didn't ever come back to Barra."

Donnie didn't want to be interviewed unless it was in Gaelic.

"There are a lot of Gaelic speaking people at my concerts. Gaelic is really, really important to me. My parents were fluent Gaelic speakers and my daughters speak it. I was involved in setting up a committee to start the first Gaelic school in Glasgow, John Maxwell and it has mushroomed from there. The only thing you can't do in Gaelic is join the Co-op because they don't have any forms in Gaelic. That's a wee dig, I am waiting for the form. I have been going to classes here on the island. I don't speak Gaelic to anyone here on the island because I am shy, but I do speak to my mum on the phone. I go to Ulpan classes which are based on the Hebrew way of teaching language. There are not enough people here on the island [who] speak Gaelic. My wife could speak Gaelic so I was lucky that she could teach the kids.

Scottish Independence is really important to me as well, and

I will be voting Aye. I believe that we can run our own lives; we don't need to go to committees in London to decide what happens in Scotland. It is simple then isn't it? I support local government. It is a not a vote for the SNP, it is about people voting for themselves, and it is really important that people make sure they are registered to vote. This is a really special time for Scotland. I like to wear my Saltire jacket when I play at my concerts."

One day planting potatoes Donnie's life took off in another direction. Here is what happened.

"I met Michael Campbell over in Vatersay. It was Hughie Sinclair, he introduced us. Michael was out planting his potatoes and I was helping Hughie plant his potatoes and he said, 'This is Michael, he is a box player.' That's when Michael came into the band. It was me, Calum, Nollie and Michael and we had a band, and we played away, but then it split up. And it just left me and Michael and then Andy, Michael's brother and another box player came in to play. George Macleod said come in and play in the Castlebay Bar anytime you like, and then Paul who plays the pipes, he used to come up and do a few tunes and it just developed into a band about thirteen or fourteen years ago. I don't think we are successful. I don't know what success is. I don't see it as a successful enterprise. We don't do what other bands do. We are not professional musicians, we all do something else.

The Vatersay Boys just play whatever they feel, whatever is in Michael's head transposes to his fingers - sometimes we are playing different tunes but we all play the same mistakes at the same time. We have three albums – *The Road to Vatersay, Sounds of Vatersay, The Sands of Vatersay*. No point in calling them anything other than what they are about. We do sell out concerts at the Barrowlands and we travel all over the world, like Spain and Denmark and Seville. The first time we were asked to play for someone else, we were playing at a wee dance in Eriskay Hall, and this wee guy came up to me and said, 'Eh, can you come and play at the Fleadh in Lerwick?' He was a digger on the causeway and he sent us the plane tickets. So we went, and that was the first time we went anywhere outwith Uist. I just used the drums that they had there and it was fantastic. I can't remember, maybe I got my own kit there… We don't have an agent or an agency, we have nothing. I do it all and sometimes Michael does it too. I need to give him his due. People just phone, and we pick and choose what we do. I don't have anything pencilled in and it all just comes about somehow. We play the Barrowlands at the end of the year, then this year the Ironworks in Inverness, then The Ferry at the 31st and 1st of January. We do have a website. I think we were one of the first bands to have a website, it was pure innovative but became inactive, but we are going to start picking things up. It is hard to make money from it because of all fares and accommodation. We have our jobs. We have a big outlay before we get paid. I don't really do my croft except look at it. Playing is the only thing that has been constant in my life. I have been out gigging since I was thirteen as a drummer, the singing came later."

The Vatersay Boys are one of the island's biggest attractions, a local band making a big noise in the Castlebay Bar every Saturday night. Donnie's drums, like a pounding heart, keep in time to the rhythms of the island he loves so well.

All three photographs taken in 2015 on The Ferry – a 'well-kent' Glasgow nightspot.

Copyright Dol Mikety

Brothers Micheal and Andy Campbell – The Vatersay Boys.

CHAPTER FIVE

# Songbird,
# Story teller,
# Poet

# Songbird

*Interviewed on 07.03.13*

**Mairi Mhol**

Island ceilidhs are a sure way to meet real talented singers. Mairi Mhol's sweet voice has been echoing around Barra since she was born in Bruernish eighty two years ago. The interview with Mairi Mhol was punctuated with some rare, beautiful Gaelic songs.

This is what she said.

"Yes my mum was a singer, most of the songs were about Barra and the different islands, it all depended on who was making the song and where it was set. Yes I was upholding the tradition of singing in Gaelic and am a keeper of Gaelic songs, we always try to keep the Gaelic singing. There isn't a Gaelic choir on Barra but we do meet every Tuesday night and sing songs especially waulking songs.[1] We call it *voor* in Gaelic. They are about different islands and are songs about the olden days when they did a lot of *voor* and it was a past-time for them. I will sing one of the waulking songs.

Well, it's about who was over on the island and the land, it mentions Barra, Rum, Eigg and Canna, and it mentions the Isle of Mull, and the women were working the wool. They were trying to stretch the wool. It is called *luadh*, big shawls and heavy blankets. It is still done on the island – we do the blankets."

Knowing the melodies and rhythms of the island, this is what she says about nicknames.

"I am a Barraich, and was born in Bruernish and brought up in

---

[1] Waulking songs are the traditional songs sung by the women of the island as they prepared the wool and coarse cloth for use in the home. Some of these songs included tales of love, and some could be quite bawdy.

Loch na Morna and am now staying in Borve. I was originally a MacLean and I am now a MacNeil through marriage. My father, God rest him, was called Mhol. I heard he was called this because he used to take pebbles and throw them at people. Nicknames are really important. It is just a habit of the islanders. If someone says I want to speak to Lisanne MacNeil, she is nicknamed Eppa and will answer to that but wouldn't answer to Lisanne MacNeil. Even in the phoney book you see all these *Macs* and a stranger would wonder who all these names are. You need the nicknames to differentiate the people. All my brothers are called after my dad, that is a tradition to be called after their dad. When we were young he used to be on nightshift in the wee house,[2] you know the one up at Greanhead. He used to be up there during the war on the look-out for boats and that. We had to go some nights after school up to that house either with tobacco or sandwiches or whatever dad needed. We had to walk all the way up there. It was three miles at least, and we did it after school up and down, sometimes you had a bike. We took a shortcut down by the sea and followed a track up to the house."

Of her family past and present she says,

"There was eleven of us, nine boys and two girls and we were all brought up in Barra. Well when we were babies and I was about two or three, and we were staying at Bruernish at the time, there was a man next door to us and he was the first man who taught us all to sing. He would have a few of us sitting on a bench in the house and teaching us all to sing. His name was Ruraidh Iain Bhan. He and Sorley Michael, they were always at us for singing. We didn't think anything of it at the time, we were probably glad to get away from them at the time. We didn't pay any attention, we were too young. A lot of children had good voices and we used to have singing a few times a week. We were taught a

---

[2] This refers to Mairi's dad who had to watch the coastline from a small dwelling on the hill above Cleit.

different song every time we went up to the group and it was all Gaelic songs. We were always lucky and had Gaelic and I went to school in your house. Actually when we went to school we had no English. We learned by reading your wee book in English. Some kids couldn't speak Gaelic and we taught them and they taught us English. I think it was difficult for the teacher.

I sang in choirs in the Mod. I didn't sing on my own because I didn't want to do it. You couldn't afford to enter on your own. My granddaughter should enter the Mod, she has a lovely voice.

My brothers went to the Merchant Navy, that was all there was then. They started off on a wee fishing boat and I think that helped. My father used to have a wee fishing boat and the boys used to go out with him to help him. I think the majority of the islanders had a wee fishing boat, and, yes, it was to feed families. You would give it away to those who needed it and that. The sea is so holy and Our Lady Star of the Sea[3] guides them all. Some of the boat names are named after her. The herring was really big on the island and all the women used to walk from Bruernish and Northbay and work on the fishing all day and then go back to their families.

Today all they have to do is press a button to wash whereas we had to boil a big pan of water, and we didn't have running water in the olden days. They were happy days. I looked after my family and I worked in St. Brendan's. I had ten children and I also worked. It was hard going, yes and no. It wasn't really as difficult as that. Today everyone has two of a family and I think of my day and no electricity. The weather was great then and absolutely better."

---

[3] Our Lady Star of the Sea is the statue of the Virgin Mary holding Jesus which stands half way up Heaval, the highest hill on Barra. It represents the local Catholic community's belief in the holy powers of the mother of God. The statue was paid for by monies raised by the local community who on the fifteenth of August 1954 carried it all the way up the hill and there deposited it to withstand the horrendous storms of the Atlantic Ocean. It is a symbol and beacon of hope and safety to the fishers and sailors alike.

Mairi Mhol

She shared a day.

"My typical day was I would get them off to school, and then the others would go out to play football or something, and you put the fire on then you boiled one or two big pans of water. You had a big tub outside with a washing board and you started off with your whites, then you did all your dark colours, you needed more water for the dark colours. It was good. Then the rinsing was done from the cold water tap outside, it was boiled on the big range. It was done on my own outside because the weather was great. It was dried and ironed with great big heavy irons. It was my life and I just had to get on with it.

The girls in my house are all good singers but the boys wouldn't sing unless they had a wee dram and that. There was always music playing.

St. Brendan's is Barra's hospital and home for patients who aren't capable of looking after themselves. It was good because I could speak Gaelic to them and they would have a sing song and a dance. Here is one I sing. *Thug mo mathair mi Ga'idhlig Bharraigh*

This song is about Barra and how your mother taught you the Barra Gaelic, and about the glen where you stayed, about the fishermen going out to fish, and how at the New Year you had drink, dance and music. It kept you going for the next couple of months.

My husband was a seaman, you just got on with it. My mother and father-in-law were very helpful with the kids they used to come down and babysit if we were going away anywhere special. Sometimes he would go to sea for six to nine months at a time, most of the year, and come back and find a new addition to the family! The homecoming put you off your routine. The kids loved him coming home because they knew he would have something for them especially clothes, big dolls and lots of nice things. I used to get nice presents too, nice ornaments – they had to be put on top of the big cupboard so the children couldn't get at them – and nylons and things you couldn't get here. It was like great riches. I have watches and jewellery that I guard and maybe would take them onto *Antiques Roadshow*.

Women didn't go to pubs. You went out to the social evenings, to ceilidhs. We would go to the Craigston Hall and Castlebay and Northbay Hall with a one man band and he was great. An accordion player, Pickie and others used to come. They used to do quadrilles, lancers and the highland schottische. On a Friday night we go along and do these dances at the Old Time Dancing. A lot of people go and it is quite busy. Last year I wasn't that fit. You have to have a good partner for the highland schottische. Domhnall a' Welder is a great dancer, a fabulous dancer. They are all musical that family. His dad was very musical and his brother has a band, DooDa, and his brother sings."

Cape Breton is home to Barra's diaspora with its own songs and when the island heritage group organised a visit, Mairi Mhol went.

"I went on the Cape Breton tour about five years ago to see the relations from the island. We had found one Peter John MacLean. He was ninety nine, and he took unwell at the beginning of the year so he won't make it to Barra. He was a lovely singer. This afternoon there was a recording of him doing a waulking song and he was wonderful singing. They are not young. He was my first cousin of my grandfather on my father's side. They were relations of ours and they fairly welcomed us. I found they had similar mannerisms to members of my own family. It is a bit strange. We went out on a wee boat and went to ceilidhs. It was such a pleasure to meet them and the Gaelic was just as good as

ours. They had different songs but they were Barra songs and we only knew the chorus not the verses. It went something like this, *Tha Duil agam.*"

Such subtleties exist in the Gaelic speaking world and when I asked Mairi Mhol to explain the differences this is what she said.

"The Gaelic in Barra it is very melodious. You know the difference – who can speak Gaelic from learning it, and who has always spoken it, because you can hear how fluid it is. The Barra Gaelic is lovely and the song was about how they were hoping to come back to Barra to stay but then they get married and they have to stay on the mainland, and that's it. *Each morning I wake up and hope to be in Barra but I can't come I have to stay here because I am married.* I am writing to people in Cape Breton who knew of our family and the next generation wanted to keep in touch. I am lazy in writing, but I phone until I see the phone bill. I spoke to Peter John MacLean once a fortnight until he died. His Gaelic was just the same as mine. I think it was a hard time when they left Barra and the majority of those who left were broken hearted. They were told they would be given jobs, and when they arrived they didn't even have houses to go to. The journey must have been terrible but their songs would have kept them going. I will finish with *Far Over the Mountains.*"

Mairi Mhol's singing of Gaelic songs keeps rolling on with the rhythmic movement of traditional island life.

# Story teller

*Interviewed on 07.06.11*

**Christopher Brookmyre**

Christopher Brookmyre has not yet been to Barra. Randomly I approached him via his publisher's email to ask if one of the main female characters in his novel *Pandemonium,* Ms Ross the English teacher, was based on me in my previous life after I had been asked by three other guests if it was me. Never expecting a response, I was astounded, and still am, when he responded. Two emails later he had agreed to be interviewed.

Despite his success Christopher remains completely grounded.

"I am from Barrhead just outside Glasgow, a typical west of Scotland small town where Renfrewshire meets Ayrshire. I went to St. Luke's High School and my dedication to my pals at PGS at the beginning of 'Pandemonium' was to my friends who had the good fortune not to go to St. Luke's High School. My friends are not particularly big fans. My pals are those I go to see St. Mirren with, two of them have read them but they are not gobbling them up as soon as they come out or anything like that. I always liked to write, my favourite part of the English class was writing a short story and I never chose any other option, whereas my pals would go on to describe going to the baths in Barrhead Leisure Centre – it must be the most written about leisure centre in Scotland – but I always wrote a short story.

Brookmyre is a Scottish name, its origins are from the Borders I think. Obviously it sounds vaguely German, and maybe if you go back a couple of generations, but I think we are Scottish going right back into the last century. My mother is so proud and never misses an opportunity to crowbar my name into the conversation – that's what mothers do. Morrison's don't sell my books, the supermarkets are a bit skittish about what they perceive to be bad language, and there is irony in that they don't want their customers to pick up books where they are confronted with swear words but loads of murder is alright.

My mum was a teacher and I read all the time. She always said that the kids that read a lot you don't need to teach them English, and the kids who don't read you can't teach them English. So I always had my head stuck in a book and English was my most rewarding class for that reason. At secondary school I wrote not so very short stories and I was involved in the debating society. I would have to write speeches and I was obviously taught the technical tricks of how to be a good speaker, like pausing and that, but being able to write a very good speech was a good starting point. I think in a lot of cases it is just there is a compulsion to just write and to create. I mean, I see in my son he is always writing stories or drawing comic books. Some kids want to consume fiction and are happy with that, but whatever he is doing he wants to create. He is always making stop motion animation clips with Lego with his wee cartoons. I think you either have it or you don't. Technically it can be taught, but the impetus is naturally there. Certainly it was always there with me. As soon as I had finished reading a book I was always wanting, thinking how could I tell that story. Something highly derivative of what I had been reading, but as soon as it had made an impression on me I wanted to do something similar."

His first steps in the reading ladder obviously enthralled his love of words. Climbing the first rung he said:

"First of all, it was probably *Asterix* making an impression on me when I was very young because it was very anarchic and energetic and always had some outrageous puns, but when I got a bit older I don't know, we didn't have the whole genre of literature aimed at older children. You know, when I was that age we didn't have Philip Pullman and J K Rowling. We had some very anarchistic books aimed at children and probably written about the Second World War, or written in the sixties by people who were in their sixties. So I found them very unsatisfactory and probably moved after *Asterix* at eleven or twelve to reading Douglas Adams and Ian Fleming. If you probably took those two elements you would have the essence of my work – *James Bond* and *The Hitchhikers Guide to the Galaxy*.

These are endless sources of inspiration for me. There is a great cliché that says you should write about what you know. I have a great belief that you should write about what you love, what you have an enthusiasm for, or about what you love to hate. For a long while I was wanting to satirise things I was really angry about, but sometimes it is just whatever peaks my interest. For example, *The Unsinkable Rubber Ducks*. I had read so many books about mediums and psychics and how that whole area of pseudo-science would make a great crime novel because it is about the same principle – trying to get away with a deception. I have always liked the patter, not just Glaswegian. I have always liked dialect and am interested in the variations and what the slang terms are."

I remembered seeing Chris during our days at Gilmorehill so I asked him how the novel writing all began.

"I went to Glasgow University after fifth year and studied English Literature and Theatre Studies for four years, and then I went to London. I met my wife at university and we were together all the way through. I worked for *Screen International* which was a cinema trade paper. I was there for four years and then my wife and I moved back to Edinburgh. My wife is an anaesthetist, she was working in Edinburgh Royal and I was working freelance on The *Scotsman* and the *Evening News* and while I was doing that I was working on my fiction. In fact, I would take two months off each year to write a book. In fact, that's why *Quite Ugly One Morning* is a tight read because I had to get it written quite quickly in the space of about eight weeks.

I wrote four books before I got an agent. It was the *Scotsman's* film critic at the time, a man called Angus Wolf Murray, he read some of my work. He read *Quite Ugly One Morning*. He quite liked it and gave it to his cousin who was an agent. He couldn't guarantee she would be interested in it, but she was an influential agent and only took on four or five new clients a year, so it was really just an opportunity. It came off because she really liked the book, and within a couple of weeks we had a deal for two books with Little Brown. I have stayed with Little Brown for fifteen years and fourteen novels.

I am forty-two. I think I was twenty-six when I first got a publishing deal and I think I was approaching twenty seven when I was published. It was quite young to be considered a writer. Because writing is an old profession, you are young if you are writing in your forties. Having started so young I thought I was undergoing an apprenticeship. I was naive enough to think that an apprenticeship ends, and that I would be qualified at some point. But when it comes to writing you are never fully qualified.

No, I didn't write speeches, my debating didn't really survive outwith secondary school, plus my recollection of Glasgow University was there was definitely a cultural disparity between the GUU and the QM – the QM was definitely the more left wing art student union, and the GUU tended to be posh kids and rugger players. So I naturally gravitated towards the QM.[1] A good indicator was those wearing faculty scarves, because they always thought they were in *Brideshead Revisited,* they tended to be kids who had been to posh schools. You certainly didn't see anyone in the QM wearing one.

Although I studied Theatre Studies it didn't influence my style of writing. Some writers are a bit snobby about who influenced them – like James Joyce and Pliny the Elder – and don't want to say they have been influenced by what they have seen in the cinema because they regard it as a more vulgar art form. But I am quite happy to admit cinema has been the most influential

[1] GUU represents Glasgow University Union and QM represents the Queen Margaret Union. In the late 1980s both unions represented opposite ends of the political spectrum with the cool lefties opting for the QM and the more reserved opting for the GUU. This differentiation between them may indeed only have existed in the minds of the students themselves!

art and narrative form in the whole of the twentieth century. It has influenced people's story telling enormously, and it certainly influenced mine; theatre not so much – there is a certain irony that I am not missing. I have just finished a book, and twenty years after graduating my degree has been of use as it does deal with the world of theatre, and my degree came in handy.

My favourite film would be *Die Hard* because there was nothing quite like it. Now there are lots like it, but at the time ... It has been imitated in so many ways – a great idea, really well executed. I would say *Serenity* has been one of my favourites over the last ten years or so. It is a science fiction movie, a follow up to the TV series *Fire Fly*."

Can writers ever distance themselves from their characters?

"There are bits of me in lots of my characters. In *Pandemonium* there is probably a lot of me in Adnam, because he is the science geek. I find the science geeks reflect a big part of me. I remember when I wrote *A Tale Etched in Blood and Hard Black Pencil* that I wrote two characters so that I could show different sides of myself and how I responded to school. One of them was Martin, and he was kind of the school swat who became increasingly embittered that the more you complete all your work doesn't mean it will win you friends and lots of popularity. Scott, on the other hand, just found something to amuse himself with every single day at school, and found the whole thing hilarious. That was the two sides to me, because sometimes I would find school a really colourful place, full of well-rounded amusing characters, and at other times I just thought I couldn't wait to get out from the small-mindedness I encountered. There are bits of me that go into lots of my characters. I have only genuinely given myself a cameo in my new book *Where the Bodies Are Buried*. It is an Easter egg waiting to be found.

The less worthy side of myself would say I indulge a bit in getting my own back, but the greater part of the exercise is about thinking about all the people I knew and considering... well...

what is behind how they conducted themselves, and try and understand why they were the way they were rather than just think I am glad to be away from that now. That's what was most interesting about writing *A Tale Etched In Blood and Hard Black Pencil,* and to some extent *Pandemonium.* There are all these archetypes on the surface who fitted into pigeon holes of different kind of school kids, but it became more interesting when you think what is behind it, and you try to subvert it. If you were at school with me you would be reading the novels with trepidation.

For that reason I am glad there have never been any school reunions. I find that, as far as I can make out, it tends to be the posh schools that have reunions. We don't have reunions at your west of Scotland comprehensive secondary, not that I have been aware of. Plus, I think having a reunion of my year would probably involve the operation of the Scottish Prison Service. Sometimes people quote me from my books and I think *did I say that in a book?* and I can't remember, being on book number fourteen now. They might have just read that book, and maybe I wrote it twelve or thirteen years ago."

Fortunately for Chris fame exists only in words.

"I don't get recognised, and I like that. I think it is the nature of the profession that writers can hide in the long grass and snipe from a distance. I think, in general, the highest profile writer will get less attention than the lowest status soap opera star. People generally can only identify from photographs a handful of writers. You could probably ask a hundred people, ask them to identify Dan Brown, one of the best-selling authors in recent history, and I bet you very few would be able to. I don't know what Dan Brown looks like, I couldn't pick him out.

I have been asked for my views on football and sometimes go on *Off the Ball*[2] and talk nonsense about football. It doesn't

---

[2] Off the Ball is a weekly produced football programme by BBC Scotland which discusses the merits and demerits of the game.

really require any particular insight. If you go into any pub in the whole of Scotland you will find anyone able to do that for hours at a time. Occasionally someone will come up and know I am a St. Mirren supporter, and, well, I might respond. But if they came up and said St. Mirren were rubbish, they certainly wouldn't get an argument! I play five-a-side and I have been playing it most of my life. I did play at Love Street because they had these fundraising games at the end of the season and you could play on the hallowed turf, get changed in the dressing rooms, and be managed for the day by the manager and the assistant manager. I didn't only play, but I scored, so I can always lay claim to the fact that I scored at Love Street which is more than what some people have achieved. I had to have a character who was not a St. Mirren supporter because I was making all my characters St. Mirren supporters and soon there would be more fictional characters than there are real ones. Sometimes they can get through the whole show without talking about football at all."

About his new novel, his previous titles and how he must always get it right.

"*Where The Bodies are Buried* is my new novel. I had a launch event in Edinburgh, in a place called The Caves, then I went down to Bath – the Hay on Wye, which is a huge festival these days. I remember I was there years ago and it was a much smaller affair. Then I was in Glasgow last night at the Mitchell [Library]. The Mitchell was exciting, but I did feel some trepidation because I was launching a book which is different from anything I have written before. It is not funny, it is not satirical, and I have not done that before. I wanted a title which suggested crime – but wasn't one of these off the wall titles that I have made my own over the years: the title sounded a bit more sombre and would tell the readers it was a new type of writing from me.

The titles just seem to stick in my head sometimes. Some of them are titles I have lifted from songs – *Quite Ugly One Morning* was the name of a song, although it was alluding to *Quite Early*

*One Morning* by Dylan Thomas. And *The Sacred Art of Stealing* was lifted from *The Sacred Art Of Leaving* by Billy Franks, my favourite songwriter. So you are never quite sure why a title sticks in your head. There have been a couple of occasions when

Christopher Brookmyre

you think *I am using that.* That was the case with *One Fine Day in the Middle of the Night* and *A Big Boy Did It and Ran Away.* It was a question of waiting until the right book came along and giving it the title. The publishers realise the titles are crucial to creating something that is distinctive from other people writing in the genre. In the question of *A Big Boy Did It and Ran Away,* I was picked up for not having *A Big Boy Done It and Ran Away,* which is how it would be phrased in the west of Scotland, but the problem for me is that I am from a family of lots of teachers, and there is no way I would have been allowed to put in the wrong use without getting years of grief from various of my aunties."

Christopher Brookmyre hopes to come to Barra one day soon.

90

# *Poet*

*Interviewed on 28.01.14*

**Donald Murray**

D onald Murray sits with a rugged handsomeness and twinkling eyes. He is a real live poet because words flow from his lips like waves kissing the shoreline of his home town of Ness in the north of the Isle of Lewis. Recently he has found success writing about the true traditions of Hebridean life. This is his story.

"I am here on Barra as part of Live Literature Scotland and have been visiting many libraries in the islands and Highlands. I have being doing a lot of work around schools, because, as you know, I am an ex-school teacher, so that is one reason. And another is I am currently researching another book called *Herring Bone* which I fancy writing about the herring industry. Barra is a vital part of that, and therefore I am speaking to people in the community. This will be a work of non-fiction, and I am laying the groundwork for that. I haven't actually signed anything yet. I have had to take on an agent, but there is a strong possibility I will be approached [by a publisher].

I was speaking at a meeting in Lincolnshire the past wee while, chatting about the guga, that wonderful noble bird, not the cormorant which the Barra people used to eat from the bottom of the crags. My last book was in the *Guardian* top ten nature books category. I have been very lucky. Will Self has picked up on my books and it is great. I met him in Shetland and I had a two minute conversation with him. He told me he liked the St. Kilda story, and I told him about my book. He told me to get my publisher to send him one, and low and behold it got a full page in the *Daily Telegraph*. I knew he was interested in the story because he has a book based on St. Kilda. *The Guga Stone* is a book about diffusing the myths about St. Kilda that are patently not true, so my book is an attempt to dismiss those tales. For example the mail boat is a nineteenth century Victorian invention, the Parliament was a village grazing committee – only they grazed on birds rather than grass. A lot of what is written about St. Kilda is just myths. And did people actually stand on the lovers' stone? I have my doubts. It is the kind of tale the people of Barra, and from my own township of Ness, have been telling for many a long year, winding up the local tourists. Probably Janice Ross was given all these myths about the place, and was probably gullible enough to believe, and didn't know the island people were sharp witted enough to tell them. This is what the book is about.

Wondering how a wee boy from Ness gives words such life he said:

"I have always been a writer. Writing comes from understanding the broken world. Leonard Cohen sings about the crack that runs through everything, that's how the light gets in, and in a way we are all fractured and vulnerable. I started writing in due course for that reason, and I think I was very lucky in getting myself into print. I entered a competition for the *Dandy* when I was about eight, and I used to win all these torches from the *People's Friend,* so much so our house could have turned into a lighthouse any day of the night! There were other competitions. I had my first short story on the BBC World Service when I was about twenty two or twenty three, I wasn't very old. So in that sense it was quite remarkable, most people are into their thirties.

I am from Ness in the very north of Lewis, a small village called South Dell. We probably have more writers per head than anywhere else. Norman Campbell and Alastair Campbell were brought up just along the road from me, a huge number of people who were song writers and other things, so there it is –quite a remarkable village.

From a very young age one of my head teachers singled me out and noticed I had a talent for writing and would enter me into different competitions. I remember the RSPB [Royal Society for

Protection of Birds] had one and I won a wonderful book with gorgeous illustrations. I think it gave me a love of wildlife, pretty seabirds not just to eat. I wrote a play for Scottish community drama while I was at school and I think it was within me. I think I was very fortunate that some of the teachers in retrospect did foster that ability.

My early life was slightly fractured. It was my dad who brought me up, my brother and I. My brother Alan is a lover of the sea and goes out sailing and kayaking. We didn't have many books, it wasn't a very literary household but we had things like the *Readers Digest* condensed books. So there wasn't a great choice of books, but I got books from the library. I think there are a lot of story-telling habits you pick up from listening to other people, and if you come from a village where there is a very strong oral tradition then I think that helps. It is present in all the islands, it was an ornamentation of life in the islands. There weren't many material goods like paintings and that but there were other riches, so you ornamented your life with language; story-telling, poetry and the song. I think this is a Hebridean thing. I think I inherited that tradition."

At secondary school in Stornoway Donald shared those traditions with all the island boys.

"For us boys it was quite a traumatic time because we left home at twelve and went to the Gibson Hostel in Stornoway. I think there was a fair number of Barra Boys there. They used to go up to the hostel. It was very trying. There were seventy-four boys and there was a lot of bullying there and a very structured way of serving the sixth year boys. I didn't particularly like that way of doing things. There was always a pecking order but, having said that, even to this present day my best friends are the boys I went to hostel with because you shared your adolescence together. In the first few years there was the common bond of suffering, and then later on there was a common bond of laughter, and we got up to things. I probably had my first smoke in their company, my first glass of wine, and sneaked off to escape their company to get my first kiss. Wandering around the harbour and the castle grounds was where we hung around.

I didn't particularly shine at the Nicholson.[1] I found the transition very difficult in the first few years, plus there was an upset in my family at that time and I found going away from home very, very difficult. There were subjects I was poor at, like Maths and Science, but loved English and History. I shone in these subjects when my creativity came to the fore, and I had a great teacher called Tom Clark to whom I owe a great debt. He could see my talent and tried to foster it by encouraging me to take subjects like drama. Come to think of it, schools these days don't have time for these subjects. In a way these days, because we are laying down so much, in a way we are achieving much less. Teachers used to do things in their spare time, now it is all about form filling. It is far too bureaucratic and I think it is about time we restored to teachers that time. I think it allows people to develop. I have a remarkable focus due to my early years in teaching. I remember looking at some papers and seeing that I had the heaviest load in the whole of the Western Isles. I took a peak and I thought no wonder I am buckling as a teacher."

Assuming his talents landed him a worthy university scholarship Donald's journey was more circuitous.

"After leaving the Nicholson I went to work, and went to night school and that was great – I got a few more Highers. My first job was as a trainee manager for Woolworths in Kilmarnock Road in Glasgow, and all I can say is no wonder the firm went bust. I was there for a very short time but they probably made a huge loss by the amount of *pick and mix* I used to steal! That was my first time away from home. I then worked in the social security in Glasgow.

[1] The Nicholson Institute is the biggest secondary school in the Western Isles. It is situated in Stornoway, the main town in Lewis. When Donald attended it took in all the boys from all the Hebridean islands and many lived in hostels. This was before the islands had their own S1-S6 schools.

**Donald Murray**

I think I was the worst civil servant ever. I was definitely a square peg in a round hole. But that was a frightening job at times. You would have people coming in and asking for supplementary benefit for some items, and you had to use your discretion. After that I went to university and found it very liberating. The fact that I was older than most students brought a terrific benefit to my life. I remember Philip Hobsbawm and people like that, and had Alex Yearling as my tutor. I did Scottish Literature too, and I think I made the wrong choices there too. I had a real talent for history and I dropped that after first year.

I decided to be a teacher and went teaching in the Nicholson. I was told I was going to Barra, but I ended up in Stornoway. There are great benefits to working in a big school in that you can exchange ideas with other teachers and follow on a tradition and continuity – there are huge advantages in that. I think the workload was pretty severe, but it also had fantastic advantages, and I used to get through an enormous amount of work. It is still part of my life today, but during this time I was writing very little."

Stories of teaching workloads are all very well but how Donald's muse returned to perch upon his shoulder was much more interesting.

'In many ways the point about waiting until later life before you write is that you have more to say. I think that I was almost silent for a couple of decades. I wrote my first poem at Lionacleit beach when I was in my forties, and suddenly I realised I could do it. At first I wrote in very traditional forms, the sonnet and other forms, but once you learn the forms then you let them go, let it flow. Now I am less strict about metres and that. I start sentences beginning with 'and'. It is only by knowing the rules that you can break them. Norman McCaig used to say when someone asked him, 'How long does it take to write a poem?' and he would say about two fags. Normally when I am writing a poem it is about two fags even though I don't smoke. It doesn't take much time once you get the rhythm, once you get the voice, then the poem is quite easy to write. There is also the musicality in the prose I write, you have a lot to draw on. When I moved to Shetland I was approached by Birlinn to write the story of *The Guga Hunters*. I had been publishing short stories and poetry in various magazines and from *The Guga Hunters* a television programme was on about the Ness men going across to an island in Sutherland, and it was a huge traverse to get the birds. I was talking about it, and I was on telly with David Attenborough telling him about the sounds of the gannets on *Birds Britannia*. An LP inspired by the book has been made.

I am exploring different fields and the book I am most chuffed about is *On This Rock,* about the Italian chapel in Orkney. I think that is really good. *Small Expectations* is about growing up bilingual and making choices you don't really know you are making. You opt for one language over another. A lot of Gaelic speakers do that without actually being conscious why you are making these choices, like in 1964 when the telly came in. It was a complete shock in the village, and it probably affected my choice in choosing English. I can't rationalise it, why I chose what I did.

Even someone coming from my background makes choices to get educated and go to university, and sometimes making those choices you don't have the full knowledge of why. As a school teacher you see children who are dragooned into making choices that are not good for them but suit their parents. Bilingualism, I chose to write in English instead of Gaelic. I could quite easily have written in Gaelic. I made one choice over the other and it is a mystery to me. *Small Expectations* is after Pip whose whole life is about a chance encounter. In a whole way it is an experience all bilingual children experience.

My other book is *Weaving Songs.* It is about the Harris Tweed industry, and my father weaving at the loom. I just sat down one day and wrote about my dad who had brought me up as a single parent, and it was as if a dam had been broken. I was very young when he died. I have been on my own a long time. Out of that one poem came a whole book. It was the hundredth anniversary of the 'Orb' and Brian Wilson of Harris Tweed he helped a great deal in getting the book together. It's a beautiful book and I worked with Caroline Peacock, a Glasgow photographer, and her work and mine seemed to fit. My poems are about the people, and I write through the female point of view as much as I write through the male view. I think that there is too much made of the differences between us."

The textual beauty of Donald Murray's word patterns would make his dad proud.

CHAPTER SIX

# Priest, Spark, Trade Union Bark

# Priest

*Interviewed on 23.06.11*

Heavenly forces brought Father John Paul MacKinnon to guide over the parish of Star of the Sea in Castlebay from St. Mun's in Ballachulish, Glencoe, and within a few weeks of arriving he had become a television star of the BBC's successful show *Island Parish*.

Shortly afterwards on a swelteringly hot July afternoon I found him autographing books and t-shirts for tourists and, as if by divine intervention, he stopped for a chat.

Of the fame the programme has created he says this.

"I didn't think when I was in Glencoe there that I would end up coming to Barra and appearing on *Island Parish* and being involved in filming. I have been thinking of getting a PA to answer my calls because I have been quite busy this past while. It is becoming quite common now that I am asked to sign autographs, and when I go to get a paper it usually takes me ten minutes. The other day it took me an hour and a half. If I step outwith the confines of the chapel house I meet so many people and they want to say they have enjoyed *Island Parish* and could I share some thoughts about the island with them. The church has that beacon, and people are drawn to it, and yes, I tell them that they have come to a beautiful island. I don't know about fame because people usually come to me because I am a priest, but now they come because of the show, and it is nice because it has been positive. I think it was worthwhile doing the show because at the time I was worried about who would watch it. I have been totally amazed by the amount of people, and just how far and wide it has reached.

I think when I was told about the programme I was a bit worried, thinking about makeup and all that, and would there be vans to do my hair and everything. But no, no it was nothing like that, no eye shadow. It was so low key they just took you at face value. I think that is the beauty of the programme – it took you as you were, no pretence. If we came across like that then it just shows a relaxed attitude. The people about were good. They didn't make me feel uncomfortable or anything. I can only be myself and I hope that is what came through. The cameras would work round my timetable. There was nothing intrusive, yes, I just took it in my stride. Certainly the programme got me known round the islands very quickly, it is a great ice-breaker, and people will now stop and chat about it.

The programme exaggerated some things, but it is half and half what was true, because when it comes to the kitchen it is a place I don't really like to be in. Using the oven is not really my thing. If I am hungry I will eat nothing elaborate but I will cook. The programme did make me out to be a bit hopeless and that's quite good because you get the sympathy and all that. I love it when people pop in a pot of soup, some scones, some pancakes and that. If I can avoid cooking I will avoid it. If I get invited out for dinner I most certainly will go to save me being in the kitchen. I will cook, but I don't get any enjoyment out of it. I come from a big family of one brother and three sisters. My mum was a fantastic cook. I think I was kind of spoiled. Everything she put her hand to tasted so wonderful. I didn't watch and learn, it was given to me on a plate so to speak, and you ate it. When I was leaving home and studying at the seminary you had people to cook for you. So for seven years I had people cooking for me. Since becoming a priest I have learned to cook, but some people enjoy it – hence we have chefs – but I wouldn't want to be there when it reaches boiling point and all that, no no it is not for me. The simple things like chopping an onion, I just do it in my own time, but you see these chefs going through it in a second. But it was entertaining learning from others. If you are on your own there is not the same impetus to cook. I love other people's cooking and I love other people cooking for me.

The programme has been good for me to get to know people

of all denominations. It has its good and bad points. For the whole island it has been wonderful. I have been in every household in one night. It was an interesting experience. I thought about if *Island Parish* were to be made into film I would choose Brad Pitt to play me! Embracing what is just around the corner is key. But my family hammer me down and say don't let the fame go to your head, and I have parishioners who quickly ground me and that is the beauty. I am just a humble priest and I have done my bit, and I have done my bit for the media, and I now just want to get on with what I am supposed to be doing."

Father John Paul's ecclesiastical compass always pointed heavenward and this is what he says.

"I joined the priesthood because from an early age I always had a sense of vocation. I knew that this path has been laid out for me, but it took other people to notice it. I was quite comfortable at my parish at St. Peter's at Daliburgh in South Uist. I was an altar boy and felt very comfortable around the church and got to know many, many priests and they inspired me. When they saw me they would tell me, 'There is a path being laid out for you.' I distanced myself from it because I was going to be a professional footballer. I am just going to play all my life, but there were no football scouts coming looking for me, and there was always this thing burning away in my head. My mum asked me if I had ever thought of becoming a priest, and if you don't ask the question the seed is not planted. It took my mum to ask me that question and I went away thinking no, no that's not for me, but it was like a light switch going on. I started talking to priests and there was this thought always burning away and I thought I am going to go for it. A priest said, 'Go and discern.' That is what the priesthood is all about, discernment. You go and you are not a failure if you leave after your first year, or leave after your sixth year. Go and embrace it, and maybe the Lord will guide you, and so I went. I approached my bishop to tell him I would like to become a priest, and asked him if he could advise me about what to do. He agreed to accept me, and sent me off to embrace the first year of seminary in Spain. I thought I could like this because coming from South Uist the idea of going abroad is mind blowing, and the bishop said yes I will accept you.

I just loved it. The studying was great and everyone around me, all the young boys from different parts of Scotland, were great. I had a fabulous time. Learning from other people who were also discerning at the time helped, and there were some who didn't finish off and some who walked a different path. Through prayers of people from Daliburgh and South Uist who prayed for me, it guided me along until I was ordained a priest on the twenty fourth of June 1999, and I have never looked back. I have always felt a sense of vocation. If you say yes, doors suddenly open and everything happens for you, that is how it is. I am now ordained eleven years a priest, and feel very happy about it. Long may it last.

When you are studying to be a priest you do your degree in Spain and everything is in Spanish, so it was a great leap of faith for me. It was either sink or swim. I had to take a crash course in Spanish and keep learning. My professors spoke to me in Spanish, the students were all Spaniards from different parts of Spain, apart from the Scottish boys, and it was really tough. The first few years you can't understand how difficult it was, translating and thinking about things in a different way. You are surrounded by it on television, the radio and you just get into it. You went for a coffee, it was Spanish, so you had to take it in. By the end of my seventh year I did the degree. It was tough learning bits of Latin, of Greek and of Hebrew so that you can read the early scriptures, and if you want to take it further you can. It certainly broadened my whole mind and horizons. People say you have to study for seven years, wow, but it is a long discerning process because you want to take as much time as possible. So I did, and gained so much information. The language is a challenge you can overcome, and now when I go on holiday I go round the different parts of Spain, not your holiday destinations, and it is beautiful, the culture and everything is great.

My mum and dad are really happy having a priest in the family. They are both devout and have a great love of the church and the priesthood, but it was not something I was pressurised into. It is something that fills them with an inner happiness that no words can describe. They have given me so much support and care and love. People sometimes wonder where priests come from, and sometimes they think they are handpicked or at a special school or unit, but I come from an ordinary family. It just comes from a loving family, all that nurturing and support. So I am blessed.

Before coming to Barra I was happily living in Glencoe, in Ballachulish, in the chapel houses there, and in St. Mun's and the Good Shepherd church in Kinlochleven. I was there for five years. I liked it, it is a beautiful area. Glencoe was always a place I had passed through going to get the boat. I had never stopped even for a cup of tea, and then I was posted there and the people have been so good. I was very very happy there. Before that I was up in Kingussie for three years, in Aviemore, and when the bishop told me I had to become the parish priest of Kingussie, I said I need to go and look at the map. I didn't really know where it was. I knew they had a shinty team. Living there looking after Aviemore and Grantown on Spey was beautiful. The Spey valley is lovely. I had a few attempts at skiing, all good fun, and luckily I didn't break anything. I went to a couple of shinty games and I really saw real shinty country.

Some of the games between Kingussie and Newtonmore, my two teams, were really tough. I really loved going along to see the games and offering my support. It is very rough, but thankfully there is a referee. The game is fast and frantic and the sticks are high above their heads, but it is like any game if you know how to play, you can ride the challenges and jump over the sticks. But it is fast and frantic. I wonder how they need a goalie because the balls just whizz past.

Before Kingussie I was down on the Clydeside at Dunoon. I was the assistant, and I lived on the Clyde there at Our Lady and St. Mirium for a year and a half. I have moved about quite a bit between the Clyde and Highlands and down to Glencoe and now up to the islands. So I have really been round beautiful parts of Scotland. The scenery and the views have been breathtaking. My grandfather was from Barra and I knew one day I would come back to the islands because it is in my head and in my blood. When I heard it was going to be Barra, I thought my grandfather came from here and I have friends here and relations. So I love the island very much. Living here has been an answer to my prayers. You just don't know where you will go, my bishop makes my decision. I would never in a month of Sundays ever have thought of Kingussie or Glencoe. I thought of other places and when I heard I was coming to Barra I was delighted. I can go backwards and forwards on the ferry to South Uist.

I am just a blank sheet. I can open my head and my heart to wherever I am sent. I am happy wherever I go. Otherwise you will be disappointed waiting for your right parish to come up. I know I will be moved again to another parish. We are obedient to the bishop and he looks around the dioceses and sees when a vacancy arises if our gifts and talents can be used in a more rewarding way. The bishop is the one to decide and that's why when I go to a parish I give it a hundred percent, because it is where the bishop wants me to be and I don't want to be anywhere else. I just think I am here and I give it my all. We give our obedience to the bishop. On our day of ordination, he says will you be obedient to me and my successors? Within the church we have canon law, and lawyers who specialise in interpreting it. If you feel you want to stay in a parish and it is part of a five year plan then you talk to the bishop and he will listen to what you have to say. He might say, 'I will leave you in the parish' you want to be in. It is one of the hard things about the priesthood, moving on, you really love people and you have to move on and say goodbye."

If the cardinal points had veered in a different direction, Father John Paul says:

"I was hoping to play for...teams with a saint, St. Mirren or St.

Johnstone. I was great at football. In Spain there is this whole Spanish football thing going on. It has taken over the world. I was really lucky to go and see Barcelona and Real Madrid and they have great players. I go to the local football matches when I can find out the times of the games. I did suggest that the times be put in the *Guth*[1] but sometimes the weather means they chop and change. I want to go along and support the local team. I used to play for Southend, so there would definitely be a conflict of interest. I will stand on the half way line with a foot in both camps and shout, 'Come on Barra, Come on

**Siar FM**
**Barra & Vatersay Community Radio**

Janice's guest this week on Barra Island Discs is a star of our television screens and a would be international footballer. Listen in and find out how Father John Paul Mackinnon, the cool and savvy performer in front of the cameras, handles the hot seat in the radio studio and describes how he spends his time when he is not signing autographs and having his picture taken by his many fans! A few surprises in store!

*Tune in to Barra Island Discs on www.siar.fm.*
*Monday, Wednesday, Friday and Sunday*
*3.30pm, 10pm & 4.30am (following morning)*

Southend', and hope it is a draw. I am sure people would say, 'Father you either support one team or the other, hopefully it will be Barra.' I would love to go and support them more often. I have retired from playing."

Father John Paul might not be a television star or a star of the football field but he most certainly shines in Star of the Sea in Castlebay.

---

[1] The *Guth Bharraidh* is the local weekly paper prepared by and printed in the offices of Voluntary Action Barra and Vatersay and serves to keep the community of Barra and Vatersay up to date with latest developments affecting the island – from changes in council policy to ferry timetable changes. The *Guth* published a short synopsis of all the guests on Barra island Discs along with a photograph of them.

*Spark*

*Interviewed on 01.05.12*

Hec MacLean is Barra's electrician. Tangled among the island's wires it sometimes takes him days to free himself. Like the sandy Barra beaches, Hec's list of customers stretches for miles...he explains his popularity.

"It all started when I went to work for myself in 1994. I had so many jobs on and I just couldn't cope so I tried to hide. I have been very busy since I came down [from Stornoway].

I was born and brought up in Barra, in Borve on the west side. When I left I was seventeen. I went to Stornoway and served my time up there. I was up there for eighteen or nineteen years and then I came back down in 1994 and struck out on my own. You always come back to your own, and I have been here since. I went to Craigston School, then to Castlebay from first year to fourth year, and I left and went to Stornoway. I went to Lewis Castle College for a year to do engineering, but when I saw a job advert in the *Stornoway Gazette* looking for an apprentice electrician, I applied for that. Four of us were taken on, and I think we are all still working as sparks. The other three are off-shore. I am the only one who is not off-shore. I like my way of life and sports and that. I am planning to go off-shore. Maybe by the end of the year I will have got my survival certificates and that. There are three or four electricians on the island. I get stopped all over the place and then I forget who I was talking to last, and then people phone up and say you haven't turned up and I say I will eventually... I always thought I would be a joiner, then an engineer, but being an electrician suited me best. Most of the boys go to sea as engineers, then joinery is the second most popular trade. I think it has to do with the fact that they take things apart and then want to become engineers. Yes, the island people have to do their own stuff, so that may be why so many of the young males go to do these things."

Being busy doesn't stop Hec from wiring up the bright flashing lights and strobes. Donning his Status Quo outfit of denim jeans and jacket he hits the decks for the young people of the island. This is what he says.

"Well I run discos because when I came home there was no-one to do discos for the boys, and I was approached to see if I would do them. A guy called Charlie Donnelly asked if I would do discos for them, that was way back in 1995. I used to do discos for them in Castlebay Hall, Northbay Hall and Vatersay Hall. I am still involved with that now, even though I am kind of cutting back. I am getting too old to do them. The type of music today I am not too keen on. It is a generational thing. The music the young people listen to today doesn't make any sense to me because music moves on. I don't like the garage music and there are no classic songs that people will remember in years to come. No one will remember these songs, and that's why I have kind of given up. Only yesterday I was in the school and they asked me if I would put on a disco for them, so I suppose I will to keep them happy.

The first disc I bought was a picture disc of Status Quo's *Caroline*. That band was way ahead of their time in their day, and they started the whole Levi denims and jacket thing. I had Levi jeans and jacket and was a long hair type of person. *Down down deeper and down*. Everyone gets up to dance to this and *Living on an island*. I like different sounds. I like country and that, and The Vatersay Boys. I like the Dire Straits' *Walk of Life*. They were Princess Diana's favourite band. Pity they broke up. To go away to a concert is a lot of planning, and I feel I have a lot of responsibility to the school as I fix all their problems, so if they ask me to do a disco I try to help out."

Before returning to light up the island with his music and lights,

Hec married the girl of his dreams, and also took over training the island's successful football team.

"Catriona is my wife who is from Lewis, on the west side. I met her in the bar at a community hall with a band called Island Express, and we were dancing to them. They were contemporaries to Runrig. I didn't see her for four weeks after that, and since then we have been together ever since. We have been married since 1984, twenty eight years married. Once she saw me she said, 'That's the one for me, and there is no getting away from it.' We got married up in Stornoway and came back here for every holiday. Catriona's family are all there in Lewis. I like Don Williams and Catriona is my *Gypsy Woman*, in fact it would be great if he could come up here and do the decks at one of our dances!

I used to practise with the football team when I came back on holiday, and in the eighties I used to have a couple of games with the boys through into the nineties. I used to do the junior football team for about eight or nine years because there was no Barra FC at that time in the league. I started off in 1998, and in 2001 we reached the cup final, but we lost to Southend United and I stopped then. Someone else took over, then Lye, the BT man, he took over, and I was giving him a hand but in 2007 he left and I took over in 2009. Then Tendai Mutembira, the chemistry teacher, helped since 2011. I am still the Barra FC manager. In total I have been doing it since then, and that is twelve years. If you include the years I used to help Hec MacInnes back in the late nineties, it is a good eighteen years. I was nominated for an award in London, but I was too busy to go down. I think it was Alan Shearer who gave out the awards. He is another hero of mine. I have a statistical mind when it comes to football. I know who has played who, and how many goals they have scored and that. I always wanted to be a football manager and a coach. When I was up in Stornoway I played with Stornoway United, I was actually a goalkeeper. I played for Barra first in 1974 in goals. I can still get a game yet, although I am now a trained referee. I like football. I wanted to be a coach and teach youngsters to bring out the best in them."

Clearly passionate about his love of the beautiful game, Hec nurtures the home grown talent.

"We have good players here on the island, like Craig Ferguson, Screech [Steven Davidson], Neil Sinclair, and Deege Wilson is coming into a great game as well. And DA [Domhnall Ailean MacLean] my own nephew, he is quite good as well. There are some very good players on the island just now. I reckon if they were on the mainland they would make it big because they have the skill and that, but the location makes it impossible. Jock Stein was great and so was Billy McNeil, a great manager if he had carried on. He went down to Aston Villa but he didn't make it then. I love Kenny Dalglish, he is still a great manager and Alex Ferguson. I think I was looking at these guys and thinking I could probably do that, and we have done that.

Last year we won a cup, and Barra had never won anything for forty-three years, so even this season we are hoping to win the league. It is looking pretty good. We set ourselves up that week thinking we have got to win this cup for the island and the community and we knew we would get a large crowd. That night it just rained and rained and we went down onto a sodden wet pitch. It didn't make life easy for us, so it brought us into extra time, then penalties, and we won the cup.

It was forty-three years since that was achieved for Barra. I was quite proud myself to have won that cup, and proud of the players too. As I say maybe the treble this year. I stand at the side of the pitch because of the trees, they give me shelter and I can hide from everyone. The other team had won the league, Iodchar Saints, they had won two cups and were looking for the treble, and had t-shirts saying treble winners, but I kept telling the players, 'We have got to win this game.' It was so wet and we lost a goal just ten minutes from the end of the second half, lost a crazy goal and I was thinking here we go again, and then Neillie Boy [the Barra goalie], no-one will ever forget that goal, made a brilliant shot that went right into their goal and that took us into extra time. Then onto penalties and we win 5-4. Then everyone just ran onto the pitch – it was like Hampden Park – it was brilliant, young and old running onto the pitch. It was a pitch invasion. I remember when Neillie Boy scored everyone came onto the pitch and it took the referee, ages to get everyone calmed down. When the final whistle went, the pitch it was just full of people. I have never ever seen that before.

The boys take it serious, they do a lot of training and they don't even go drinking on a Friday night like people used to do. They take it serious, they want to win and they will be successful. Last year they went to Clyde. Robert Ross organised it for us to play with the under nineteens. That was an eye opener for us to see their set up. What we have got is totally different, you know, and like I say we saw a couple of managers at Clyde and a couple of players and they were impressed with our boys. Our location to send boys away for coaching is just impossible. The boys play for the whole island community for Barra and for Vatersay and they play from the heart. There is no one playing for themselves. Every single one of them has a sense of responsibility to the whole community which makes my life a lot easier.

The problem with the football team is kids going away to college. See Iain Beggs and Mish [Michael MacInnes] going away, they are big misses and Iain Nicholson working for CalMac, they are all a big miss. Iain Nicholson is a great strong team player, and if we lose we lose six points. The Davidson boys, there are seven of them playing, and they are all good players, Mary and Christina's boys. Sander is coming through as a great player even though he is still young yet. Neillie Boy is the main man and is probably the best keeper in the league. He is really good and has been there for about the past six or seven years, and he is the best keeper. He always gets called up for the Uist and Barra Select. Some of the boys – James, Craig and Neil – are all playing for the Uist and Barra Select. They are wee boys playing in a man's league. At the moment we are second in the league, and if we win against Iodchar Saints on Saturday we will reduce their lead to two points, but Saints are the top team. They are the ones to beat, so hopefully we will come back with three points and it is away. To lose to Saints will open an eight point lead.

Steven Davidson was Man of the Match for me last week– he reminded me of Jimmy Johnstone – and he is sorely missed when he is not there. He is like a wee Jinky. We keep a note of all the Man of the Matches, and me and my assistant tally it up at the end of the year and have a Player of the Year award. Last year it was Mish [MacInnes], he was Player of the Year. There is no-one to beat him, he is great. Neil Sinclair got Young Player of the Year. He is just wonderful when he is on form. Deege Wilson is a cracking player, and I am sure he will be a great player. James Davidson has been the main goal scorer. We get large crowds now. COME DOWN TO WATCH OUR GAMES, WATCH THE BOYS IN ACTION."

Hec MacLean no longer manages Barra FC but the boys continue to go from strength to strength. Hec MacLean has trained as a referee and does not show any bias whatsoever. He is still a hard man to get hold of.

Hec MacLean and his winning team

Janice K. Ross

# Trade Union Bark

**Bob Crow**

*Interviewed on 01.03.11*

Caledonian MacBrayne[1] has always provided a life line to the island community and when the Conservative Government decided to steam ahead with plans to privatise their routes many families felt threatened. The late Bob Crow, the General Secretary of the Rail Maritime Transport workers happened to be in Castlebay for one night and held a meeting with his members. He agreed to meet me for an hour the next morning before heading up to meet members in Stornoway.

This is what he says.

"Well actually this is the third occasion I've tried to get to Barra. Our members in our union on Caledonian MacBrayne operate

© Janice Ross

these islands and we represent them and once a year we do a trip to speak to the members and speak to the people in the communities. This is the third time lucky. On the first occasion there was such bad wind the plane wouldn't take off. The second occasion was last November when we was hit by the bad snow and weather, and today I'm in Barra after flying yesterday from Glasgow on probably the best day of the year so far – not one single cloud in the sky. And absolutely breathtaking scenery flying over all the islands and coming to Barra. The experience of landing on a beach was something exceptional.

Yes, we do believe there is a danger to our members' jobs. What is happening is that the European Union has decided, and we don't believe that the Scottish Government should abide by what the European Union's saying, is that the routes that

[1] Caledonian MacBrayne is a publicly owned company which provides the necessary ferry services to the Hebridean island communities and those on the Clyde estuary.

Caledonian MacBrayne operate – in fact it's one company that runs the highland services, but is split into four separate packages, there's round about twenty-five different routes that operate – and as result of that the European Union say that they should be tendered. Tendering has told us over the last twenty years that when they are tendered other companies come in and try and cost cut. The things they try and do is cut our members' pay and conditions and also try and worsen the services. We believe it's wrong and that's the reason why we're campaigning against it. Some five years ago the same thing happened. And with the communities in a broad movement amongst the islands and the workers that worked on the services, we've managed to push back the privatisation of Caledonian MacBrayne.

Twenty percent of the thousand people that work for Caledonian MacBrayne actually come from the highlands and islands itself, and there's other people that obviously originate from the highlands that work there as well. So it's a massive employer. The community service as we see it is not just about taking the tourists around, which is obviously essential for the economy of the islands, but the service is more importantly a lifeline service to provide a community with all of the kind of provisions it needs. For example, recently in the Isle of Man they ran services to Liverpool, Dublin and Heysham, just north of Blackpool. A company turned up called Meseron from Estonia who ran a cut-throat service which cut the pay and conditions of the staff that worked on the Estonian ship, and basically what they done was they tried to undercut the Isle of Man Steam Packet Company which was devastating to the Isle of Man community. After weeks of campaigning they've disappeared now, and the Isle of Man have got what they want – a good service. Now we're not saying by any stretch of the imagination that the services can't be improved. They should be improved. But last time the Scottish Government spent £23M on a tendering process. This tendering process was one of lawyers, consultants, and we believe that £23M should be spent on new vessels and more services for the islanders."

Listening to Bob was enthralling, his powerful delivery was mesmerising, but I wanted to know more about him personally and to find out what made his clock tick. I asked him about music.

"I love Al Jolson. You have probably got two lots of community at the moment. Some people would not actually remember him but would remember his music. His name actually was Asa Jolson. He was a Jewish lad from Washington who run away at fourteen years of age because all he wanted to do was sing. He sung in the synagogues and become a fantastic singer, and he was disowned basically by his father who was a leading rabbi of the synagogue. But he ended up in a place in New Orleans and the music he was told to sing wasn't the actual music that he wanted to sing. But in them days with racialism real rife in the United States of America, the New York jazz men couldn't go out and sing in white clubs so their music was very, very secretive. He managed to go into a few clubs and this is the way they sing, and he adapted his music so when he was singing he was actually singing how the black people sung from the Deep South. That was Jazz, basically Jazz. He was the biggest person who actually moved jazz on, it was Al Jolson.

I'll do a little bit of song for you."

At this point Bob sang a medley of Jolson songs word perfect.

"Al Jolson's records used to play on a Sunday morning in London. The pubs only used to just open from twelve to two on a Sunday. Now they're open all day. Just like in Scotland years ago when you had to come from another part of the city, you've got to be drinking in the same town, as where you usually drink so pubs used to be shut except twelve to two. My mum's day on a Sunday was cleaning the house. She used to put her records on. So did everyone else in the road by the way. She used to put her vinyls on as she used to call it. And in the summer time the windows would be open and you would hear music all the way down the streets from different people. There would be Tom Jones playing or Englebert Humperdink. My dad would be over the pub, and I would go and meet me dad over the pub, and he'd give me a bottle of coke and a packet of crisps and I thought I was in heaven."

Castlebay Hotel was populated with top officials from CalMac who stopped in their tracks as this giant of British trade unionism opened his heart and filled the room with his warm melodious tones.

"I like a whole variety of music really, you know. It's the music I like first of all without the singer, but there's some real talented people about over the years when you weigh it up. I mean Tom Jones, I like Tom Jones. I like Phil Collins, Genesis, Supertramp – a fantastic group, Spandau Ballet, Amy Winehouse – fantastic – and Duffy, I think she's a fantastic singer, Lily Allen – another fantastic singer. There's some real talent about. And, you know, I'm not a person who likes the operatic songs but Kathleen Jenkins is another fantastic singer. So there's a whole great range of singers at the moment. I mean, one of the greatest singers I think, so underestimated, and I forget her name now, but she sung in the *X-Factor* – she was the Irish girl who worked in the supermarket. I'm just trying to think of her name. Mary Byrne! And I thought she was absolutely fantastic when she give it the big numbers! I think she was fantastic. So all kinds of music I like really.

I love karaoke, yes, there's nothing better than a good karaoke. I think once you've had a good drink and get up there and sing *Sweet Caroline* or *Hands*, you know *Crackling Rose* – all by Neil Diamond. It's always worth a good sing-a-long."

Loving finding out this hard man was really a big soft karaoke king, I wanted to find out how he had become one of Britain's most feared men.

"Yeah, we come from basically near Tower Bridge station actually,

Tower Hill which is basically the City of London now. It was a place called the Minories, but it was a staunch Irish community. Basically East London had two communities. It had the Jewish, which was basically north east end like Whitechapel and Stepney. And then you had the Irish, that was basically Shadwell, basically the Irish encompassed the dock workers, and the Jewish moved into Whitechapel which was the Tailor Trade. I mean when we say about north and south we're talking about three-quarters of a mile from each other. But in them days people didn't travel. You know it was a bit like the island communities really. Everyone knew everyone. And as a result of that the two communities entwined very well. The Jewish and Irish communities got on extremely well. There was no battles between the two of them. In fact they complemented each other. The Irish used to basically run the pubs. And the Jewish people used to do the food at which both of them met together. In fact fish and chips is a joint Irish/Jewish tradition. The first fish and chips shop comes from about a mile from where I lived, and basically it was the Jewish from Eastern Europe that come up with their bad fish. It was a Spanish-Jewish tradition, and the Irish had the fried potatoes and the two of them entwined to have fish and chips – one of the most famous dinners in the world!"

Bob's rhythm was picking up pace so I let him go on, clearly delighted to be sharing these magical moments.

"I spend me time like going to the gym six days a week. I like the gym because I go to the same gym and I speak to the same people in the sense of the word. I know the people down there, and we have a good chat and a good laugh. It's not one of those gyms where everyone's worrying about what you wear and you've got to look designer. You can put on what you want and do what you want. If you don't fancy training so much one day you can sit there and watch the television or read the papers. I love the gym. Good people down there.

My favourite pastime is watching Millwall Football Club.

I mean they're my life and my death. I'm sitting here with my Millwall watch on. And I love Millwall to death. I also like watching the TV. You know I like watching documentaries. I like watching comedy. I am even a soap king. I watch *Eastenders*. I watch *Emmerdale*. And I watch *Coronation Street*. I don't watch them religiously, but I like to keep up with what is happening. I listen to all music, listen to all TV. It's nice just to relax for an hour or an hour and a half, or even walking in at night time at eleven o'clock. I couldn't go straight to bed, I'd have to sit down for thirty five, forty minutes just to unwind and watch the television. I think television is a good way of unwinding.

And yes, I do read books. I should read more than what I do. My eyes are getting a bit worse than what they were. I don't wear glasses yet. But it's coming to a time when I'm going to have to start wearing reading glasses soon for some of the words - they are either printing smaller or my eyes are getting worse. I read all kinds of books. I do love autobiographies. I must admit, autobiographies are my favourite. I'm not a fan of science fiction. I don't mind a science fiction film like *Star Trek* but that's as far as I can go. I can't get into this *Aliens* thing but what I do like is autobiographies. We've got a fantastic library. And it's under threat at this moment in time. The local library is only half a mile from where I live, and its stacked with books in there, and they're very good because if there's not a book in there you can actually order one, and because London's got so many libraries, and the Central Library, you can get your book within seven or ten days which is very good."

Notoriously known as a private person he says:

"Well that's not really true in that sense of the word. Really no, I just don't get my family involved at all in what I do. I mean I've got four children. Two of them are schoolteachers. One works on the railway and the youngest one is training to be a midwife. I've never told them what they've got to do for employment. The four of them have never brought one ounce of aggro home to me whatsoever which I think is a great credit to them. Not like me. I brought the aggro home to my parents, but I mean they have not brought one ounce of aggro home. And what they do as well, I tell them you know you've got to make their own destiny. I don't tell them how they should vote. It's up for them to make their choice. But I've got to say that what I try to tell people, what I try to instil into them – and it's the only thing I've instilled into them – is, 'Treat people like you want to be treated yourself.'

No, I can't get to nightclubs anymore! Come twelve o'clock me head hits the pillow, I'm afraid. I might be able to push it at a conference to half past twelve or one o'clock, but come twelve o'clock me head hits the pillow."

Talking about his job he says:

"I mean on the main I'm out of London twice a week. I am. I'm responsible for the administration of the Union and not just doing meetings. I mean, there's no one back at the headquarters who's actually responsible for taking control of the administration. There's people who do the administration obviously for me, but I'm actually in charge of the administration. It's good because at the end of the day the members want to see their General Secretary out and about. They want to speak to you. And I think it's good that, you know, you don't become too cosy in London because you can lock the door in London and think the problems ain't happening out there. But you need to get out there and start speaking to people, and you learn so much by going out and meeting the members. That's what you learn from. And I actually really love it. If someone could do all the administration work I would go out and do meetings five days."

When I asked him how it felt to be on the Tories most wanted list he laughed, joking that there would need to be a pretty high ransom before anyone would turn him in.

He said:

"Well I suppose they hate you really. I mean you know the Tories have an ideological hatred against working people. They've never wanted working people to have anythink. They don't want us to have decent housing, decent education, hospitals and schools. I mean, look this morning what's happened. I mean in the medical world, which absolutely amazes me, the brilliant scientists there are now, and they've just come up with a new test that basically can pinpoint prostrate cancer. This new test they've got is only going to be available…eh…if you're private. Now I think it's absolutely scandalous that at a time when they've just given millions upon millions, in fact billions upon billions, to the bankers they can't give money so people can have a decent prostrate test. To me that's unfair. And they're the sorts of injustices that we need to fight against. And of course the Tories don't want any kind of Trade Unions. They want you to basically doff the cap to them. We're in charge.

And I've always said to managers of companies you know we don't want to do your job. You are the manager. And we respect you for being the managers. You're the employer and we're the employee, but you should be able to treat people with dignity and respect."

How did he see the future panning out?

"Well the fallout of the amount of money that's been given to the bankers is now evident to be seen. That's why we see high inflation, high prices. They call it 'quantitive easing' and 'derivatives' but they're just words to baffle working people really. I mean I've never heard of quantitive easing before. I didn't know what it meant. Years ago when a new word came out it went into the Concise Oxford Dictionary and it would be on the national news. A new word is out today. This is what this new word means. All of a sudden the word 'derivatives' comes up and 'quantitive easing'. They're not the sort of words that I use.

You know I hardly get home at night and me boy has just come back from doing a night shift. And he says *hello dad how is your quantitive easing today?* Or, *have you got any derivatives for me?* I mean what it basically means is that they're printing money. That's what they're doing. They've lent money from people in the form of bonds and they've given it to the Bankers. So they've really given money which they haven't got. What that really means if you've got a hundred quid but you owe twenty pound to someone it's not really worth a hundred pound, it's is only worth eighty pound. So sterling is falling and that's what's causing inflation. But who knows what's going to happen? Because, you know, I'm not a pessimist, I always like to be an optimist with people. I like to think people have got some hope out there with all the despair they're going through. But to me things ain't improving out there. I don't think things aren't getting worse in the economy. Everyone can speak for themselves.

I think things are trudging along the bottom. And who knows what can happen?

I mean a lot of these Western governments are jumping up and down about Gadaffi.[2] And I'm certainly not supporting Gadaffi. I couldn't give two hoots about him. But it seems strange to me that only a couple of years ago that Blair was hugging and kissing him and saying what a great bloke he was. He's come back to the West. There was this dodgy deal about getting Ali al-Megrahi[3] back from prison into Libya, and then all they're talking about is the exploration of oil that's going on with British companies in Libya. He's a nice bloke again. A friend of the West! All of a sudden in a couple of weeks he's against the West.

And it seems to me the only thing that they're interested in is oil. Because well, I've got to say, it's scandalous what's happened

---

[2] At the time of the interview Colonel Gaddafi's leadership of the Libyan people was under serious threat from various opposition forces. Having ruled the country since 1969 and nationalised the oil industry since then Gaddafi's idea of Islamic socialism was considered a threat to world order. Shortly after this interview he was found murdered.

[3] Abdelbaset al-Megrahi of Libya was accused of the Lockerbie bombing which killed 270 people. He died protesting his innocence.

in Libya. It's scandalous what's gone on in Egypt! Why aren't they saying anything about Kuwait? Why aren't they saying anything about UAE, the United Arab Emirates? Why aren't they saying the same things about Dubai? They're all undemocratic Governments. He's not saying nothing about them. And of course what it all boils down to is that they don't mind a tin-pot dictator so long as that tin-pot dictator supports them. Just like Sadaam Hussein was a friend of the West until he turned into Frankenstein and then they turned against him. There's been a number of United Nations resolutions against Israel. Where's the attacks on Israel? It seems to me that any government that's friendly to them they're prepared to accept. So who knows what can happen? I mean if oil hits $200 dollars a barrel which is not going to stop me frightening people. That's what people are saying in the financial papers, that oil could hit $200 a barrel. That means doubling the price of oil to what it is now. That would have a massive effect worldwide. Anything could happen in the form of a worldwide recession.

Just imagine what the effect would be if that doubles. I mean it would put off, no it would severely ruin, the industries that operate here, and it would put off loads of tourists from coming here as well. And…ah…it's obviously the problem that you've got where we've squandered all of the oil in the North Sea. We've still got the oil in the Brent Oil Field and there's still some production. But production's at its peak now in the North Sea. And all them years that Thatcher was in where she spent all the money, basically from oil, to keep people on the dole queues when the Norwegians banked all their money! So when oil runs out they've got decades upon decades of still continuing with a good standard of living for the working people of Norway."

Outside the hotel window the *Clansman* was manoeuvring its way alongside the pier. Almost mirroring its actions, Bob slowed his thoughts right down and brought them home to Barra.

"Yes, there's fear for jobs. I mean, you know, especially talking to the people last night from the Barra community, basically their industries are built on maritime whether it be Caledonian MacBrayne, or whether it be the oil industry supply, or fishing. It's what the community has built up here and obviously our people work in other islands and they base the trade. Hopefully this year…eh…there will be a few more tourists than last year will come to the islands. And it's a shame really with Barra because the services to Barra are pretty poor. I mean to get from Oban to here is four and a half or five hours. Or you go to Glasgow and there's only one plane. It's a shame because if it could be opened up like the discussion we had last night that services… we shouldn't be arguing should the service go from Barra to Mallaig or Barra to Oban. There should be services to Mallaig <u>and</u> Oban that's what we should be looking for, that's what we got to be campaigning for! And more services every day. And I think meself this is a beautiful island. And it's a fantastic place to come to. And I think meself this a golden opportunity to actually tell people what Barra is all about. It's one of the islands that people don't know a lot about to be fair. You keep hearing people say go to the West Highlands. They talk about Arran. They talk about Mull. They talk about obviously the beautiful place of Oban. But Barra's a beautiful place as well.

See the problem is, with people coming into the industry, young kids coming in – any young kid coming in to an industry wants to know that there's a bit of future for them. At the moment in time what happened was that the Labour government brought in what was called the Tonnage Tax and the Tonnage Tax was to get more ships to come into Britain. When they used the British ports they would pay a tax, but part of the tax would go back into the industry to train apprentices. That's a good step forward. But what the Labour government didn't do – and it has been a success story that British ships are using British ports more now than ever before – but the problem has been that they're foreign flagged ships with no British, Scottish labour on them whatsoever. And what's happened is that we've seen some officers being trained, such as cadets, but all the able seafarers, the people that have the ratings, there's been no training being done whatsoever. There's only two areas now basically where it happens, and that's Caledonian MacBrayne and a bit of the Royal Fleet Auxiliary. Apart from that there is no training of cadets going on whatsoever because what these companies are saying is that…well…Number One people don't want to go from school anymore because they're frightened that their jobs will be taken away from them by foreign nationals. We're not against foreign nationals. It's that the companies in other countries use and exploit that labour to undermine the agreements that are in countries that have got better pay and conditions. As far as we are concerned, any nationality can work on a ship so long as they get paid the same terms and conditions as what the collective agreement is with the employer. But if people don't see there's a future in it,  that's the problem that we've got. And, you know, what we're trying to get back to is where we was years ago, were you now going into the shipping industry. I mean, the old seafarers who you see there last night - some of them forty, forty five years. Once they've gone into the shipping industry they have near enough stayed in the shipping industry all their life. The problem is now that the job security is not there any more, and that's the problem that we've got. But we've got to get these young kids back involved."

I asked Bob how his own life had developed.

"I left school at sixteen years of age with one single exam. But it was a different world then in 1977. I could have got a job in the Gas Board, the Water Board, and Ford's. I could have got a job on a building site. I could have got a job anywhere I wanted. In fact there was no pre-requirement to do well at school or to go to college. If I had wanted to be a bricklayer I could just go and get an apprenticeship and do one day a week at brick-laying. By the way, I'm not knocking school. I played football most of my life at school. I used to bunk off and go and play football and cricket and rugby. I liked school. I liked going there. I liked the social side of it, but I didn't like sitting in the classrooms, to be fair, and when we was given opportunities, for example to have a free lesson so you could do what you want, we used to go and play football. And then they started saying we could have double lessons of what we liked. So we was playing football and cricket for half the week basically. But it was different. There weren't the pressures that are on people now. Now kids have got to do so well at school even to get into university. If they go into university they've got to be funded, outside of Scotland, to a massive amount of debt which puts another massive stress on them. And then they've got to try and find a job after. Where the problem at the moment of time is, not whether there's enough university places, it is there's not enough jobs for people when they come out of university.

I started in London Underground when I was sixteen. I was a Junior Railman, and you weren't allowed to go onto the track where the electricity was until you were eighteen. My job was come in the morning, getting there early actually! The work, the gang started at half seven. My job was to get there at seven and make their tea for them and then make their tea for them again at ten o'clock, and then go down the bakers and get their rolls for them, and then put their bets on for them. I was only sixteen. I used to go in there and put their bets on with a bookmaker. Put their bets on for them then come back and do their tea for them at lunchtime. And then run any letters to the office. And that was my job for the day. It was a fantastic job. And of course all the lads used to do overtime and one thing or another. If you were under eighteen you weren't allowed to work on the track. Believe it or not, my job was watering the plants at the London Transport head-quarters at the weekend which was a fantastic job. You was given a key to walk around the Broadway. And at sixteen years of age I used go into the chairman of London Transport's office and sit in his chair and sit back. He used to have a garden and at the back of his garden there was a garden pail and I used to water his plants. I thought this was incredible. I'm sitting in the chair of the chairman of London Transport's office at sixteen years of age. I've watered his plants and I loved it.

I got a job in my part of East London, and in fact the TUC General Secretary at the time, a man called Len Murray, he lived in the road next door to where our gang met, gang worked. He used to come in and start chatting to us on the platform and chat with us. Very friendly bloke. Len and I weren't involved in the trade unions at all until I had a row with my 'ganger' the foreman. And out of vindictiveness he sent me to Rickmansworth. Now I thought I was going to Japan, so I thought how far away it was. I didn't realise I'd be coming to Barra some thirty years later. You know, but he sent me to Rickmansworth which was only about an hour away on the train. And I was being paid overtime to go there as well.

And I said *this ain't right*, I'm being victimised here, and I went down to me branch meeting. Firstly my branch meeting was on a Friday night at half past seven in a small pokey, smokey hall in London. All I remember now was all these old blokes sitting up on the platform, probably like me now. I was looking up at them and I thought *Christ, this is boring or what!* I told them what my complaint was. One bloke said, 'Well serves you right!' I thought you was supposed to be helping me, and in the end I got my point of view over, and what they said was, 'We'll have a word with someone.' I think they just said, 'This is only something small here, we'll sort it out.' And then they asked me to come back to the next meeting, so I went back to the next meeting. All me mates used to go out on a Friday night and they asked me where I was going. They laughed when I told them a branch meeting. They was all out gallivanting with women and one thing and another, and here I was going to this branch meeting. When they asked me to be branch secretary I agreed to do it but not on a Friday night. I basically revolutionised things with a small 'r'. I changed the branch meeting to a Friday – half an hour after pay day. So everyone got their pay and then went straight to the meeting. Then we used to have a drink and turn it into a social and everyone enjoyed theirselves and people could go out on a Friday night, and we encouraged youngsters down there.

I mean, life's about enjoying yourself. You know, life's not about working all day. I mean, people can enjoy theirselves how they want. I mean, you don't have to have a drink to enjoy yourself, I accept that. But the fact of the matter is, you know, if people like a drink I don't see what the problem is, that once you've finished a hard day's work or you've got a day off then working people are entitled to put their feet up and enjoy theirselves."

Realising that the hands of my hour with Bob Crow were reaching their final destination he reminded me of something important.

"I mean, you've got to be not above people. You've got to be with them. I mean, you know I've always said to people you can't be a hundred miles in front of your members, you can't be a hundred miles behind them. You've got to be with them. And I'm not one of these people that, you know… the general secretary before last – the former general secretary, come from Scotland, Jimmy Knapp who unfortunately died of cancer some ten years ago – but the general secretary before him, he used to have a chauffeur and it's hard to imagine. There would be all these railway workers there and he would get in a car and drive in his Jag with a chauffeur down to his office. The receptionist used to call him Mr Will. And Mr Green the General Secretary before him. When I started as general secretary the receptionist's name was Keith - lovely man – and I walked in and he said, 'Good Morning, Mr Crow.' And I said, 'Keith if you ever call me Mr Crow again you're on a discipline. You call me Bob like I call you Keith.' I can't stand snobbery. You know, I can't stand that at all. I can't stand it in people in the union because we're all members and we're all comrades. How people get above their station, to be honest with you, I can't stand that.

Well I mean people who go to private schools and university they have never really frightened me. I mean, my mother used to say there is only one university out there, the University of Life, and she's right! These people who've come from a private background – I'm not knocking people who come from a private background at all, that's their life, but they haven't...they're not street-wise. If you notice about them they can't come in and socialise properly with working people. In fact they try and make out they're working people, and you know some of them try and dress like working people, but they stick out like sore thumbs. So my belief at the end of the day, you know, is treat people how you would want to be treated yourself. But at the same time it doesn't frighten me because someone's been to University and they've got this and that and the other. You know, I think meself that at the end of the day all you got to do is put your hand on your heart and think...know what's right and what's wrong. As far as I'm concerned I can put up an argument against anyone, just because they've had a private very elite background doesn't stop me."

Having just a minute to go Bob still found more words for the community.

"I'd like to say thanks for the fantastic turnout we had last night at both meetings. It was a shame really that the two meetings clashed, but fair play to the first meeting – which was held by the island's Council and Caledonian MacBrayne, which allowed me just to have five minutes at the start – because we wasn't trying to compete with that meeting at all. The first meeting was about trying to see with consultation whether services should go to Mallaig or Oban, or what kind of services there should be. It was quite clear at the meetings last night that they purely wanted one thing and one thing only, and that was the services going to Oban. There were some fantastic comments made there as well about extending the services to Mallaig and so on, and I think that's been taken on board.

And the second meeting was regarding the privatisation and the people turned up fine. I mean last night, when you look at it for a community of probably what twelve hundred people, I mean take London's got six and a half million people and if we had the same percentage of people that turned up in London last night as the same percentage of people that's turned up in Barra, well even the Olympic Stadium and all the other associated buildings wouldn't be able to hold those people. So it was a fantastic turnout, and it was clear what the islanders wanted. They were opposed to the sell-off of Caledonian MacBrayne and the break-up of the industry. I'd just like to say thanks for the hospitality and warmth that was shown by all the Barra people that we met all day yesterday. Our next meeting is going to be in Arran, and then we've got a further meeting in Stornoway taking place. I do a tour up here every year of the Caledonian MacBrayne members. It's always been a problem getting to Barra because it takes so much time out of the schedule. I'm certainly going to be coming back to see the lovely island of Barra and the lovely people of Barra as well."

The tick met the tock on the face of the clock and my lifetime of an hour had come to an end. But what a lovely, lovely man!

**Castlebay, Isle of Barra**

# CHAPTER SEVEN

# Teacher, Councillor, Minister

# *Teacher*

*Interviewed on 16.03.10*

In 1964 a young teacher from Eoligarry, Peggy MacCormick, was interviewed by Magnus Magnusson for a documentary *Disappearing Island.* However Barra and Peigi are still here and four generations of the island's school children have passed through her hands, gaining unique insight into the folklore that shapes island life. This is her story.

"I love Barra. The thing is you know everybody, you know most people on the island and you all have a similar way of life, that sort of thing.

I am completely a Barraich. I was born and bred in Eoligarry. I live in Earsary now, but Eoligarry was my original hometown. My mum and dad went down to Eoligarry in 1920 as a load of other people went down at the same time as sort of pioneers and that is where I was born and brought up. Eoligarry was actually, something like the same idea as, you know, the raiders in Vatersay. People went to Eoligarry because they had been promised land. Various young men of that era had been promised land by the government. It was like a pioneering thing. The department bought the land from the MacGillivrays who owned it, and it was divided into forty crofts, and I think it was that you picked a number and that was your croft. My dad picked number twenty five and that was our croft. So that was how Eoligarry became a wee township. I believe Eoligarry was called Flogarry Flois because it was a name that meant it was good for breeding cattle meat and that. I used to think the name was a Norse name but it wasn't, it was a Gaelic name, Flodigarry and it became Eoligarry. My brother has actually written a story about how the people went down there."

Peigi is a crofter…of sorts…

"I don't know if I would call myself a crofter. We have a croft in Earsary. We used to have sheep but we no longer have them as we are getting on in years. But we do have peat and my son cuts the peat and we use that, and that's about all. Someone uses the land for cattle grazing and that sort of thing. There is a croft in Eoligarry and that is the main croft where I was brought up. I inherited that croft from my brother and I have passed it on to my son. It is a nice croft there and it has been used to grow potatoes, it's just for our own use to plant the potatoes, grow them, pick them and eat them for ourselves, just like everyone else. You know it is beautiful machair[1] land down there with rich sandy soil. My son is developing the land a bit, but hopefully this year we will have carrots and things. In the next croft to us, Victor's, he had strawberries and everything; I was quite envious of the things growing there. Well that's it.

Crofting is really very important, but you can't sort of live off it. When my parents were living down there my father had to go away to sea and earn his living that way. You couldn't exist on the croft alone, but it is such a wonderful way of life. We had our own milk when I was a child, and things like that. I think it is very important to maintain the crofting way of life, the crofting existence."

Peigi just always knew she was going to be a teacher.

"Yes, I wanted to be a teacher ever since I was a young child. I used to stick cans on posts and pretend they were pupils, and the embarrassment when I noticed someone watching me. But yes, I have always wanted to be a teacher. I am not saying that I am a good one, or that I was a good one, but I did always want to

[1] The word 'machair' is Gaelic, meaning an extensive, low-lying fertile plain. 'Machair' has now become a recognised scientific term for a specific coastal feature, a type of dune pasture that is subject to local cultivation, and has developed in wet and windy conditions.

be one. And when you talk about the number of children I have taught, I have actually taught – they talk about teaching someone's children, but I have taught someone's grandchild [laughter], the granny when I was teaching at first then the grandchild when I was teaching on supply.

I went to Castlebay School for three years then we went to Inverness Academy. I liked it there. We lived in Hedgefield hostel. I made many friends. There were girls from Harris and North Uist. And from there we went to Glasgow, Notre Dame, and spent three years there and the people there were lovely as well. Well, I started teaching in Brevig away back, I won't say when – in the year dot. That was my very first post. Actually it was 1960 I started teaching in Brevig and spent six years there. I left then and went down to England for about four years but came back again when my son was born. I have lived in Barra ever since, and that's it.

After Brevig I taught in Craigston. I already had two children by then, and I taught there for twenty-three years. I absolutely loved it. I loved all the schools I taught in. But I was so long in Craigston there was something special about it. The children were wonderful. It was a lovely community as well. I just loved the area, and that was it.

In actual fact, Craigston was such a Gaelic community, there were many Gaelic speakers there, and I used to get patted on the back because there was a bilingual policy going but it wasn't my teaching, it was because they were speaking Gaelic in the home so it wasn't difficult to have Gaelic spoken in the school. It was easy, and so we didn't teach through the medium of Gaelic all the time but we did do a lot of Gaelic. It wasn't a Gaelic medium school but we did use it a lot."

Gaelic singers, story tellers keep the folklore traditions alive, Peigi is no exception to this.

"Well my mother was a story teller, she used to tell us a lot of stories when we were children, Barra stories or otherwise and I used to enjoy telling the children stories and they loved listening to them. Well, it was great in those days because, well nowadays you have to have permission to take the children out anywhere – all the officialdom that has crept in – but in those days if the weather was good and that sort of thing you just made use of it. Craigston was in an absolutely fantastic setting and you could either go up to the dùin,[2] right up the hillside, or you could go along the beach, or you could go along the stream. We used to do a lot of that and make use of the environment and area. Some stories I remember of the fairies, the dùin over there and that the fairies lived in the hillside, that sort of thing. You could get the children to believe in these things.

You see there is just something special about the islands. I just can't explain it. I know that we don't always get good weather here, and that sort of thing, but there is just so many stories and songs to keep me company. To be quite honest I just like living on the islands and that's it."

Cathy Ann MacPhee, the wonderful Gaelic singer, sings the same stories in song.

"Cathy Ann is my niece and also my goddaughter. I was in my last year in college when she was born and I just remember it very well. Yes, she has sort of made a name for herself singing. My mother was a great singer but I don't think any of the family inherited my mother's voice but Cathy Ann did and she sings beautifully. She's a great character; she has a wonderful personality as well as having a beautiful voice."

There's a warm and a knowing smile that radiates from Peggy MacCormick that makes you think she does indeed know where the fairies live.

---

[2] Dùin represents mounds in the hillside.

# *Councillor*

*Donald Manford was interviewed twice but this transcript is from our second interview on 27.08.13.*

Donald Manford

D onald Manford, since I have lived here, has been its elected councillor. He campaigns to safeguard the fabric of the community. This is his story.

"I certainly didn't set out to be a councillor. I was probably yelling and demanding that something get done and I saw that people were pushing me, and some good people who assisted and directed me. Most of them are now dead. I very strongly believe in my heart that I want the community to attain more decision making powers and controlling our own lives. I am a Barraich.

I was born on the north end of the island in 'Stupid Street', that's the old name for the road where my parents and grand-parents lived in Eoligarry. My people expected to be given land when they returned from the First World War, effectively they were not given the land they were promised so they squatted along the shoreline, building shacks and makeshift houses. At the big house the gentry would stand and discuss what 'these' people were doing, calling them 'stupid' and everything. Eventually they were able to remain on the land, and the street was also referred to as Stupid Street. My father was Welsh/ English border farming stock and was in the Air Force, and my mother was in the Women's Air Force, and the rest they say is history.

My mum's family always came from Barra and she was Nellie MacKinnon. She was in the Air Force as ground crew assisting with the landing of the aircraft. Isn't it wonderful how gender politics have moved on? My mother wanted to make a contribution to the war effort. It wasn't unusual for women to move off the island and the herring industry is testimony to that. Island communities are remote, but island communities don't have a remote mind –far from it. I don't know what selection process took place or what motivated my mum into the Air Force. Many island people who were in the war want to talk about what they did. She would talk about the camaraderie during the war and how people stuck closely together during danger. It is the case that island people will not disagree to the point of no return because at some point there may be a dependence on those people the next day, and I think that is instinct.

They were in Lossiemouth and got married in Elgin, then moved to Wales and stayed there for a number of years. They were both working there, they were quite settled, but came back to the island when my grandmother fell ill. But for that I may well be a Welshman. My oldest sister was born in Wales. I am the middle child and there were nine children. My Welsh sister has moved back to Barra. Some of us are in Barra, one in Uist, one in England. We are scattered about. I don't really know what made her stay. She is a founder member of the Council of Social Services and had an interest in the community. My father joined the Merchant Navy and like many other men travelled the world. That is something an island community has always been used to, and that is why the females of the community are so assertive in getting things done because they had to when their men folk were away at sea. I see the womenfolk don't have the same standing as men in other communities, and Barra is richer for the women's voice."

When it comes to voices Donald is no stranger to the ceilidh floor.

"I like to think I am a sociable person and it is important to relax and enjoy. I do think it is good to enjoy conversation with the people who live round about us. I try to go to ceilidhs which coincide with an event of significance for the community. I like island entertainment and I like to contribute and take part. I am a singer of Gaelic songs but I don't get as much opportunity to take part. They are as relevant today as when they were written, but my knowledge is limited. The ceilidhs of old are different from today's ceilidhs, when people would visit each other's houses during the winter and the long dark nights and the ceilidhs were a way of passing the evenings prior to television coming to the islands. There was a seismic change, and these events dwindled away."

Postponing our interview I chided him for being late and he told me this.

"The meeting today over-ran. It was about Marine Scotland. The management of the sea is very important to this community since we are surrounded by it. More and more with the coasts and the sea, the sea is expanding further beyond fishing including fish farming and aquaculture and it is becoming increasingly important to us as communities. More and more people are becoming aware of the nature around us, not just on land but the huge wealth of nature and resources of the sea. Information technology is making us aware of it and providing opportunities for employment and investment. I genuinely think we are scratching the potential it can bring to the island.

Marine Scotland is about discussion and knowledge dissemination. There are concerns and worries and there are tensions between the proposals of Marine Scotland and the working practices of the fishing community here on the island. The meeting is about information. It is not necessarily tensions about fishing, it is about conflicting interests that sometimes come about through misunderstanding and misinformation. We want a good clean sea and a healthy stock. Tensions arise regarding how things are being done and they are there because we all have different priorities and it is trying to create a balance in the community. Of course it is natural to feel aggrieved because there are people with experience who are in dispute with people whose knowledge is learned. The difficulty arises when science becomes the most important component and the question is whose truth is to be believed."

**Councillor Donald Manford**

Fighting for the future of Barra is what motivates Donald.

"In Barra it is really important to have a community that is knowledgeable and alive in the community. There needs to be facilitating of people's knowledge and skills. We too often are the receivers of something that is passed down to us by others rather than creating it ourselves. I don't think responsibility is anywhere as it should be on Barra. My view is there are no limits to the power people on Barra can have, and that power will be decided upon by the will of the people and their own capability to do things and change. Barra people have never wholly managed their own affairs, and I see wonderful things here on the island when I see young people wanting to engage more and more. You can't ask people to be responsible if you don't give them the responsibility to be so, and if you don't give it they will take it. Any community has to be skilled and of course young married people come here and want to raise a family. We should be able to afford to do that because it becomes difficult when institutions are needed to create employment. People need to have the drive to make change and create a growing thriving economy. I want Barra to be as dynamic as it can be, seeking the powers to deliver positive change for the future."

No-one would disagree.

# Government minister

*Interviewed on 10.06.11*

Alasdair Allan

Alasdair Allan and I went to university together but we never met until he came to Barra. He is MSP for the Western Isles, and is now minister for Learning, Science and Scottish Languages. Geographically and politically it is a huge area to cover. This is his story.

"Well, I am in Barra quite regularly and I try to get round all the islands, thirteen in total, although I don't get to St. Kilda as often. This is the most beautiful of constituencies. There are not many like this in the Western Isles. Everybody knows who the MSP is and gives me jobs to do, and that is healthy isn't it? The days of big public meetings are over, I think, courtesy of television but I don't think I have a job for life. I hope I work and people give me credit for that. I certainly don't take this job for granted.

I have always been interested in political issues. I have always supported the cause of the SNP, and always put out leaflets. It was comparatively late on that I thought about becoming an MSP, it was when I worked in Alex Salmond's office. I was involved in debating at school. I never studied politics but I was always involved in university elections. It was only after I left that I stood, although I did twice stand when I was a student to no avail and got kicked into the kerb. It was in 2006 that some members asked that I throw my hat in the ring for the Western Isles. I have no family in the place but I speak fluent Gaelic. I have always been a fan of the place but thought you needed to be born in the place to be an MSP. But history has proven me wrong and I am glad to be here.

I come from a wee village near Selkirk. My grandparents were farm labourers, and my parents were teachers and live in the house I was born in. My mum and dad are still in the Borders and my brother and sister-in-law with their two kids live in Musselburgh. I am not sure about reciting the Border Ballads, but James Hogg has family connections. I studied Scottish Literature at Glasgow University and did a PhD at Aberdeen University. I was born into the Borders and brought up there so I think I know Scotland. I have been in many areas of it including the very windy Peterhead. I am here in the Western Isles and I love it here."

Big areas to cover, big responsibilities.

"Well I am glad I have responsibility for Gaelic because I learned it from scratch, and if it is to survive then the figures have to become a lot less fragile. We need to set ourselves some very clear plans so that by the time of the census in 2021 the numbers will be back to the 2001 figures, which means we have to stem the decline. I also have the responsibility for other things like reform of the college sector and modern apprenticeships and improving attainment in schools.

People's concerns are wide and varied here on the islands. For example, I have been asked to find someone a replacement petrol tank for a 1957 Volvo, and I have been asked to get someone's highland cattle into the slaughterhouse even though their horns were too big for the door. I have been asked for all manner of things. The constituency things are the need for jobs, and the need to keep people here on the island. I think internet access and broadband is a huge concern and people have a right to expect this service.

Fuel poverty is very high here and people find it difficult to keep houses warm. We need to make sure that houses have central heating, and that the benefit system recognises the weather here is different and there is a huge wind chill factor here. Older people need to stop worrying about how hot their home is. There is a satisfaction to be had from solving people's problems. I can't promise the world but I will try my hardest to sort their concerns. I have a surgery in Northbay Hall. I am somewhere in the Western Isles every week but most people just come up to me and give me a problem. There was a big division in the community about renewables. The community was divided and the planning application didn't go through. That was very tricky. You are a politician twenty four seven, and when the phone goes at two in the morning you are not as keen."

Scottish Independence means so much.

"The support for Independence has become a reality and it is not only just an SNP thing but is for everybody, and the campaign seems to have made more people aware of it. I have given up having a normal life because I believe Scotland could prosper if we had a normal government. The younger people seem to be more excited about Independence and that can only be a good thing. As time goes by more and more people have seen the success of other countries becoming Independent. The key thing is there is support out there for change, even among people who are not yet signed up for it, they want change. It is about embracing change. Within Scotland people who move here are just as likely to vote for Independence as those of us who were born here. Scotland has lots of space here for new people."

Loving traditional music has always fanned his passion, and Alasdair relaxes singing lots of songs however on the day of the interview he declined.

"The Corries were among the first people to revive Scottish traditional music in the Borders. I do sing in a Gaelic choir at the Mod for the village I live in Lewis. My music is through singing and I enjoy going to the Mod. I like Arthur McCormick – he is head of Bord Nan Gael. I am a big fan of Burns and I think he is under-rated because he has been caricatured. Burns rocks. I do quite a bit of recitation during the Burns' season. It is not always Burns, it is all Scottish literature. One thing we are doing is to make sure that in the school curriculum all pupils have access to Scottish Studies. Scotland has to be proud of its national literature. I don't get much time to read but I do like Sunset Song, to me it sums up the world of my grandparents. The thing I regret about being a politician is I don't get to read as much as I would like, except for political papers. I like Derrick Thomson and Sorley MacLean. I sing as I cut peats especially if I need to learn them for the choir. I find that relaxing."

A very learned man with twinkling eyes and lots of smiles made me wonder if he was on the lookout.

"I am not married. I am on the hundred most eligible bachelors of Scotland list! I don't have a flash car or anything to attract anyone because I am driven about from engagement to engagement. I learned to drive here on the Western Isles. Before that my epilepsy was a bit of a problem. I limit my driving to a single track road. It took me four times to pass my driving test. I was behind a funeral cortege and it took up loads of my test time. I don't have great faith in horoscopes for choosing a partner. Apparently I am a Taurus, but I must be on the cusp because I am not really very stubborn, I am very sceptical. I don't think there is an SNP astrologer, not officially anyhow!"

Girls if the full moon alignment is in your chart and you are quick, you might just catch Alasdair hot on the campaign trail.

Copyright © Rachel Biddy

**Alasdair Allan, MSP**

Alasdair's counterpart at Westminster is Angus Brendan MacNeil MP who wrote the Preface for this book.

Copyright © Allan Milligan

**Angus Brendan on his croft**

CHAPTER EIGHT

# Projectionist, Activist, Scientist

# *Projectionist*

*Interviewed on 11.01.10*

**Iain McColl**

I ain McColl is a showman, a magician extraordinaire. Through rain, hail sleet and snow he brings his box of tricks to the most remote and rural areas of Scotland. Watching his box unfold into a cinema is a work of art and I caught up with him one day when he had just finished preparing his tardis for show time. *Cinema Paradiso* is one of his favourite films.

"I come to Barra every six to eight weeks. I am from Argyll, Tighnabruich, which is similar in size to Castlebay – maybe slightly bigger, there are eight hundred people there. I have been with the Screen Machine for thirteen years, since its inception really, and I have been in wonderful places. Today I am in Castlebay and tomorrow I am in North Uist, then up to Harris, and then onto Skye. How good is that? I can see the latest films many times. I am really pleased to be involved in the mobile cinema.

I have done lots of jobs and all my skills come together in the Screen Machine. It is not just showing a film, it is hydraulics, it is generators – lots of different things. I drive the truck, set it up and keep up the maintenance of it, and no-one has ever complained. It is much easier to have a wee cinema because everyone knows each other so there are never any problems. We provide a link trying to emulate big city cinemas with obviously a few short-comings. It delivers what an audience is looking for and that is a cinema experience. So we put a lot of time and research into the vehicle. People are pleased to see you, but when it is a bad film choice, I have to take it on the shoulders.

I do all my own maintenance. The lorry is like two big drawers opening out and you need to know how to open these drawers because they can't be opened at an angle otherwise they won't work. It has to be highly maintained and I spend one day a week underneath it in my overalls, just making sure everything is fine. You can't always get a signal on your mobile phone so you are on your own, but the good thing is there is usually a welder, an electrician or a joiner. In the eleven years with the old system we never missed a show which is quite a high achievement really.

Going way back it was probably the Highland and Islands Film Guild that travelled around the local villages. It was old fashioned 16mm film. I would help the guys carrying the equipment, and I had a real interest way back. A bit like *Cinema Paradiso*. You arrive in the village and you do the presentation. In many ways you are a showman, and you have to make sure the cinema is warm to relax and watch a movie in a good friendly atmosphere. I know if people are happy I have done my job and I am happy. Where we go is usually decided by the remoteness of it and the access. The truck is seventeen and a half meters long, so it is slightly longer than your artic lorry.

I used to drive trucks all about Europe so I know I can handle all the machinery. When I am off duty I still go to the cinema, and I do criticise if the cinema is not doing it right. If you have a mechanical breakdown there is a tremendous disappointment in the village. There have been times when the weather has stopped me coming to Barra from Oban, so rather than not turn up I will go round the long way via Skye to get here so that people are not too disappointed. It does cost us, but that is nothing compared to what we deliver. The lengths we go to is always appreciated. In some places today big trucks are not welcome, and I don't know what other truck is made as welcome. Some kids from school wave to us and that is really uplifting, it definitely cheers you up. I hear people saying this is such a lovely experience, and it is warmer than my house!

I spent some time in Ireland, both playing and working. They have a similar set up like the Screen Machine. They have got their Cinemobile which is based in Galway. I have been over there before we put the same idea on here, learning how it would work. I have to be a jack of all trades and you need to have a lot of mechanical skills because of the generator. We are totally self-contained, plus all the projectionist stuff is very twenty-first century as we are digital. The old 35mm is now gone but it presents new skills which are computer based. Films now come in a black box. I miss the 35mm film.

We do twenty-three different venues, ten islands and all the North West highlands, so we do a massive area. It is an area the size of Belgium, and it is a vast empty space void of cinemas. We have an eighty-seat cinema and we will help out in any area."

I thought I could do Iain's job except for the maintenance bit - quite a big bit. I could choose the films, all my own favourites, and I wondered if that's what Iain does. He explains.

"We have an office in Inverness and we choose what films we show. I have the casting vote. Some films sell themselves like *Lord of the Rings* etcetera. Sometimes we move away from the mainstream films and go for something a bit different, like when the Stig Larsen films were out there was an audience for them – not a big audience. We always have a kid's film because it is a big percentage of our audience. The whole system is financed. It costs in the region of £230,000 per year. Obviously we need a big percentage of that as box office, and without that we wouldn't be on the road. It is a year to year costing and luckily it is down as a valued asset to the small communities, and long may that continue.

If we took more specialist films they don't pay for themselves. Fifty to fifty five per show helps us break even, but less than that and we have to make up the shortfall with increased subsidies. That's the main reason why we don't go for limited audience choices. I remember we played the film *The Cruel Sea* here on Barra, and the school children loved it. Of course, the film portrayed real mariners who came from the island. So there are occasions when you can tie in a film to what is happening in the local area.

Regional Screen Scotland own and operate the Screen Machine and Highlands and Islands Enterprise fund it. The

National Lottery funded it along with HIE to build the machine. It is now Creative Scotland who fund it. We have an independent sponsor through the Royal Bank [of Scotland]. CalMac could sponsor us…

If a community wants a special screening of a film we would try to accommodate that.

The problem is that we have to give the film distributors a percentage of each seat that is sold. We are slightly behind the main releases by about two weeks. The film comes in hard drive so it is easier to use than the way it used to be."

The showman and magic box has been about.

"I took the older truck over to Bosnia for the Millennium to show films for the troops and spent six weeks travelling about. It was an amazing success and I was invited back the following year. Now the army has its own mobile cinema. The guys were in a cinema and they weren't in Bosnia and they forgot they were in a war zone. Again the audience knows each other there and there is a shared happiness when they are together.

I visit ten different islands, but leaving Barra and Vatersay is always a wrench, especially as I am always listening to The Vatersay Boys on the way out. But I know I will always be back.

My favourite time was when we showed *Mama Mia* and I was christened 'Bjorn Crazy' from the Abba movie. When the credits rolled I dressed up and did this crazy dance in front of the audience, and ice melted and the laughter flowed. It was brilliant. People have said it was the best night ever. It was a spur of the moment decision. It is a feel-good movie and I prepared by painting boots silver, searching the second hand shops for a shirt to go with the overalls which were dyed, because I just knew this was an opportunity to bring some magic into people's lives."

Iain McColl in his glad rags brought islanders to their feet. In reel time they were dancing and clapping along with the showman, rocking his magic box of tricks.

Copyright ©
AnnieM

Top –
Iain McColl – the
projectionist
christened 'Bjorn
Crazy'.

Centre –
Screen Machine
unfolded.

Bottom –
Screen Machine
inside.

2016: Iain MacColl and Neil MacDonald are still bringing movies to Barra approximately every eight weeks. It is one of the forty locations they regularly visit, with support from Creative Scotland, RBS, Highland Fuels, Caledonian MacBrayne and its many loyal customers.

Christine Galbraith

# *Activist*

*Interviewed on 16.03.10*

Campaigning for the benefit of the island is second nature to Christine Galbraith. If she finds something which will bring benefits to the people of Barra her voice becomes a mighty shoulder pushing slow turning wheels. I snagged her one day unawares. This is her story.

"I do one or two things, but not as much as other folk, but it keeps me going. Well, I spend my day in the butchers, then I have the school to clean after that, and see what the kids have been doing all day – making a mess usually. Then I am also part of Northbay Community Initiative which runs Northbay Hall and the Bothan, and keep things ticking over in Northbay. The Northbay Community Initiative was the title given to a group of people down in Northbay instigated by Roddy MacLeod and Michael MacNeil to upgrade Northbay Hall and the area around Northbay Hall, to bring a bit of life down into Northbay. It has been going now for about six or seven years – time has passed so quickly I can't quite remember. They have now moved on with their busy careers, and I have now become the chairman of that committee, and it's just as I said, it keeps Northbay Hall ticking over. We have done a lot down in Northbay and it has improved the area.

I think anyone passing through Northbay in the past couple of years will have seen what has been taking place. We work very closely with the garden project, and going by there you will see lots of new poly-tunnels. The initiative itself, with the help from a lot of people over the years, has updated Northbay Hall and the kitchen has been re-kitted out with new dishes and cutlery, new dishwasher, new cooker. It has revamped the toilets so as to also give a good toilet for a disabled person, and the ramp is there to give easy access. People who have come through the committee have done a lot of work to help us in finding the funding and the grants. Even though I am there just now with the committee, it is people who have gone there before that did a lot of the work. People are good with helping because maybe they are willing to help, maybe not on the committee, but will turn up if you are having a bingo. They will turn up with prizes, or – if it is a ceilidh – baking, and help on the night. Not everyone wants to be on a committee but everyone does want to help on an individual basis.

Northbay Wood, it was part of some quango of the government – I can't remember which one it was, it doesn't matter, because it certainly helped the north end through the project and gave employment to people who are long term unemployed. It gives employment to them. But that was a separate project, and it has been a great asset.

Iain Galbraith is my husband and is better known locally as Rusty. He works down in Barratlantic.[1] He doesn't venture out much, we keep him tied down in Ardveenish. He works down in Barratlantic, he doesn't come up to Castlebay that often except in July when Jimmy Ferguson takes his holidays and he has to take over in the fish van. So that is really the only time he gets any time in Castlebay.

Conversation with Christine is warm, witty and very, very funny. She strongly identifies with the Gaelic culture of the island.

"I am a Barraich. I was born in Oban. My dad is from Oban but my mum is from Barra, and when I was a year old they moved back to the island, in 1960, so I have been here ever since so to speak. I am a Gaelic speaker. It is very important. It is something we have always just had. We learned it. People say to me, 'Your dad

---

[1] Barratlantic is one of the biggest employers on the island. It is a fish processing plant in Ardveenish which sells various crustacean and fish to local and European markets.

wasn't a Gaelic speaker, so did you speak English or Gaelic?' And I dunno – we spoke both depending on who we were speaking to. I have always spoken Gaelic with the English, so it has just been part of our life and our heritage I suppose. I encourage my children to speak Gaelic although none of them now live on the island. They were brought up with the language.

I have two girls, Elizabeth who is twenty-seven and Marion who is twenty-three. Elizabeth is married, in Glasgow now, and gave me my first grandchild six weeks ago – a little girl, Maria. And Marion lives in Wales after graduating in Gaelic from Aberdeen University. Wise move to go to Wales!

I suppose like us all there's a man involved. She met a very nice boy from Wales when she was in Aberdeen and moved down there to find work when she graduated, and is happily settled down there. She is trying to learn Welsh. People used to say that Gaelic was a hard language to learn but, from what I can see and hear, Welsh seems a lot harder. But I think when I see how the Welsh are keeping their language alive, I think they have a better idea, because it is compulsory, I believe, in all schools rather than having a separate unit for the language. It is integrated into the mainstream and I can't help but feel they have got the better idea in how to keep the language alive."

Now Christine's girls are off her hands she decided to see other parts of the world. Here is what happened.

"We decided, after talking about it over the years, that we would love to go somewhere different. Iain had always had a longing to see New Zealand, having heard about it from the sailors who would come home with great tales. So on the thirtieth of December we left Barra, spent New Year in Glasgow and on the fourth of January we left Glasgow in four degrees [Celsius] and arrived in Singapore twenty four hours later in twenty-four degrees, and that was only six o'clock in the morning. We spent a couple of days in Singapore, it gets you used to the heat before you hit Sydney. Sydney was amazing. I really, really loved Sydney.

There was a brightness in the country, it was the same in New Zealand. Not just the sun and the warmth, but the light was so different. We just had a ball and we just loved it.

We didn't go to visit particular people but we did meet up with some people. The reason I had a hankering for Sydney was over the years we had heard about a cousin of my mother's who had married as a war bride, and I thought wouldn't it be great and so I met her when we were down there. She is now eighty-nine years of age and has a great mind, and she is able. It was so special to meet her. It was a joy to meet her family, and while I was doing that Iain skinned out of the visiting and climbed the Sydney Bridge.

When we went to New Zealand, we met some people – Iain's cousin and his wife in Wellington. It was very nice to get talking to the locals of the islands, New Zealand and Sydney, and to get their points on different things. Iain, being a Celtic supporter, wore a lot of Celtic tops over the five weeks. That was a great way to get people talking. 'Are you actually from Scotland?' Or 'Are you over here and just wearing the top?' And that would lead to other conversations. A great conversation starter.

Most folk we spoke to had a good idea of Scotland or had visited Scotland, part of the reason they had approached us. There was a funny one when we were in Talpole, which is in North Island. We were in a pub and this chap came up to the bar and we started talking. I said, 'You sound as if you might be Scottish yourself,' and he said, 'I am. I have been here for about nine years now.' So I said, 'What part of Scotland are you from?' Obviously we are from the west coast, and he said, 'Glasgow,' and I said, 'Glasgow, but do you mean Glasgow or somewhere near Glasgow?' He said, 'Paisley'. I said 'You are from Paisley, not Glasgow, Paisley,' so we had a bit of banter going then but some of it can't be repeated!"

Funny, I couldn't imagine Christine having anything other than a conversation full of banter such is her quick wit. Inheriting a penchant for reading this is what she adds.

**Christine Galbraith**

"My dad was an avid reader and it was something that we did when we were young. Dad always read to us and encouraged our love of books. I think the whole family have a great love of books, and you are talking about the one liners that are inherited from Dad. Dad was very much like that, so we all have a bit of it in us.

Well actually I would read anything. It didn't matter, if we didn't have a lot of books. I would read a book twice just to be reading something, but yeh, I would read pretty much anything. I am not saying I will finish a book if I don't get into the story. Or a new one I am trying and not getting into, I might not finish it, but most books I will certainly pick up and get into it.

Most books we just pass round the family. Kathleen is good for passing on books, and Clare, my sister-in-law, she passes books on. And when I am away I will pick something up in the book shop or in Tesco. A book club would be good. It is probably something that no one has thought about because we all go about in the same circle. There are quite a lot of readers on the island and it is probably not something that anyone has thought about, but that is how things get started, isn't it. It is just a small kernel of thought, then it is just actually getting down and doing it."

If Christine is the driving force behind it the book club will soon be a feature of Barra life.

# Scientist

*Interviewed on 03.05.12*

Professor Sir William Stewart

'Big Bill' lives up the road from me. On my way to the beach with Seumus, my collie dog, I sometimes nod hello and enjoy the interlude because he is handsome, tall and charming. A heady mixture indeed! This is his story.

"I am an Ileach who lives in Cleit. My house is at the top of the road next to the phone box. I have Murdo Beag [MacLennan] and his wife Fiona on one side, and Richard and Barbara Hall on the other side. They are excellent neighbours. The house was built by my late wife's grandfather who was called Neil Grear and it has been in the family ever since. My first wife was actually born in the house. And now Elizabeth – my first wife died – Elizabeth and I have been married for three years and we now look after the house for my three grandchildren, three boys – one sixteen, one is fourteen, and the youngest is six. Hopefully, in a few years one of them will be living in the house. So that is my connection with Barra - an Islay man, who came to Barra by marrying a Barraich who was born in the house. They were all MacDonalds. They were originally from North Uist, and they are related to Cecelia; Margaret, Ruraidh Cross's daughter; Roddy and Niger's wife; and Archie MacInnes down in number one Cleit. That's how I ended up here in a MacDonald's house.

I was brought to Barra as a newly-wed, like a prize bull. If I came today I would have a ring on my nose. I had tea in the best room, with a white table cloth and eggs and cheese, crowdie. I had forgotten my razor and there was a big debate as to whether I would be allowed to use Cathy's uncle's razor. I was allowed, so I had passed a test. I have had great fun in Barra and have been coming here for fifty years. I remember the youngsters – Alan Mhol and Mairi Mhol, and Dean and Prune who is now dead, the Gunnar and Archie MacLennan, who was a wee boy, and Ang Mhol. We had a great time on the island. We had the croft when it got passed down through Cathie's family and then we decrofted it. I don't care if the Barra boys don't like the Islay boys, all I know is that Islay boys are very tolerant of everybody."

So what was Islay like?

"I come from Islay so basically I went to school there. I am actually a Glaswegian. My father was a policeman who went back to Islay and worked in the distilleries and then became a school janitor. There were eight Port Ellen distilleries then. I worked as a plumber's mate during the summer holidays. You had to make your own tea, and milk was always carried in an HP sauce bottle. The HP bottles were great because you could plunge it into casks of whisky and keep it for dances you went to. Dances were almost every night during the summer. There used to be lots of excise men on the island and they too plunged a little. We knew they had a bottle too and used to hide it in a wall. We used to watch. And when they got to dance we skipped out and had a wee dram, but we always left some for them. In those days we danced to country and western music.

I did all my schooling in Islay until senior school because my Dad didn't think I would make it as a joiner and he told me to stick in at school, so I did. In those days you either went to Oban High or you went to Dunoon, depending on what 'foreign' language you studied. If it was Gaelic you went to Oban, and if it was French you went to Dunoon. My parents didn't speak Gaelic in the house, because my mum was from Glasgow and didn't understand it, but my dad did. So I decided that no one in the house could speak French, so I chose to go to Dunoon High and learn that. I used to say to my father, 'I can't speak it but I can understand it,' and my father said, 'So can the dog!'

I went to Dunoon Grammar then went to Glasgow University and had a great time going to dances all the time in Govan Town Hall or St. Simon's. One of the dances at Govan was called an

Emperor's tango. If you fancied someone you took them up to dance a slow smoochy number so you could hold the person close. I used to go a lot to dancing – it was the only place you could get a girlfriend. I did a degree in biology, which wasn't very macho in those days. I wanted to be a schoolteacher. I had been told by my old teacher if I wanted a job as a teacher I could come and see him, but the day I went up to see him the school had got out early. I then went to see my professor and told him I wanted to be a teacher. He said, 'Stewart you should be doing a PhD.' And that's what I did. From there I became an academic."

Becoming a specialist in seaweed Bill continues:

"There is a funny story, I used to have an old truck in Cleit and one day when I was going to Castlebay I picked up a young man hitching to the ferry and he got in. I was dressed in west coast national dress of overalls, cap and wellies. The young man was a bit condescending, and when he got out the truck I asked him what he was doing, and he was collecting seaweeds, doing a BSc on seaweeds. So I said to him, 'If you come back to Barra again you will get some good red algae on the east side, like *Gigartinia stellata, Chandrus crisus, Rhodymenia palmate,* and you will get *Ascophyllum nodosum, Laminaria digitata* and *Fucus serratus* on the west side.' He stepped back in awe and asked how I knew all that. I said, 'Oh, all us west coast men know that sort of stuff.' I hope he became a wiser and better person!

I got an assistant lectureship at Nottingham. I was asked during the interview by the professor if I supported either Glasgow Rangers or Glasgow Celtic. I told the professor I supported Partick Thistle, and that seemed to take the tension out of the situation. I went to London, then the United States on secondment. The Chair of Biology at Dundee became available and I applied for the job. I got the chair at the age of thirty-two. I was a baby professor. Dundee became a different city once the university developed and Ninewells Hospital was set up. I was a foundation professor of biological sciences and helped to build up life sciences in Dundee to its current position of international eminence, and when I was there I had a really good time. I joined the Gaelic choir and we were definitely in the bottom league of choirs. If we had been a football club we would have been relegated. We had a lot of good fun and I wrote a ditty:

> *Oft times we have travelled to Mods near and far*
> *Sang at the ceilidhs in many a bar*
> *Drunk some concoctions that set us on fire*
> *It's part of the training for Dundee Gaelic choir.*

I asked him if the government came looking for his knowledge of seaweed.

"I became a mixed biologist and from the west coast. So when the government decided they wanted to decontaminate Gruinard Island, on the west coast, where they had exploded Anthrax bombs during World War 11– one of the reasons they used it there was because it caused animal diseases (Anthrax had thick spores on it so they needed something that would withstand bomb forces, but it was so strong it lasted fifty years) – I was asked to chair a committee to oversee the decontamination. We got it decontaminated by spraying it with one percent formaldehyde, which was helicoptered in, and the rest sea water, and sprayed the contaminated area and it worked. Eventually we couldn't detect any Anthrax, and it was decided to return it to civil use, but I suggested that to make sure sheep could be used to check. Forty sheep were then counted on, and forty sheep were then counted off. One sheep did die a month later, but totally unconnected to the island. At the end of it all we had a dinner in Dundee. All the heid bummers from London, we told them we were having a celebratory dinner in Dundee! It was a British Government committee which had vets, chemists and biologists.

After that I moved down to London because they were looking for a chief executive of the Agriculture and Food Research Council. So I did that and worked on various other things, then two years later I was offered the position of Chief Scientific Advisor to the government. That was in 1990, and for five years I did that and got involved in things like nuclear fusion, nuclear fission, genetically engineered crops, and we wrote a new science white paper which made significant impact.

During that time I used to go to the Highlands and Islands Society of London which was full of Lewis people, and they would all be listening to doleful ditties from back home. I would ask them if they would go back home, and the response was always, 'Are you kidding? I love it here. When I return home they think my accent is so cockney.' Of course, they spoke with very thick accents. How many Lewis men does it take to change a light bulb? Two – one to change it and another one to write twenty-three verses of a doleful ditty describing how good the first one was!

I retired at sixty with a knighthood. The Queen taps you on the head and gives you a thing you wear round your neck. You need a morning suit and a black hat. I didn't wear a kilt. We were going to come to Barra but my wife died. Then I became a consultant for the pharmaceutical industry, and was on the road again.

I worked for large farmers and small farmers, and then the government was looking for a chair for the National Radiological Protection Board. Elizabeth, my wife, was working for the Department of Health when I went to be interviewed by her boss. Elizabeth was told to look after me until her boss could see me. She was a typical civil servant type then, flattish shoes, long skirt, dowdy hair and I was served cold tea. But the next week Elizabeth had her hair done and was wearing a miniskirt, and I got hot coffee and a chocolate biscuit! She was an oncologist at the Marsden, but to spend more time with her kids had joined the Department for Health in London. I was offered the job and decided I didn't want the job, but I told Elizabeth I would take her out for lunch or dinner. I took her for dinner and she became my second wife. She is half Welsh. She loves coming to Barra. I became chairman of Portadown lab and I took over as chair of the Health Protection Board. I did that until 2009. Since then I am quite happy to be retired and chat to you!

The Barraich say the problem with clever people is that they find new ways to be stupid! I love Barra. I think no matter where you come from if you apply yourself you can make it and grasp opportunities. I wrote this wee poem when I arrived in London:

*When I went down to London it was my finest hour*
*To be a man of substance in that emporium of power*
*They told me down in London best brains were ten a penny*
*When I got there I realised there weren't many.*

The cabinet secretary said to me, 'You must have more to do than write songs like that.' He was from Oxbridge, unimpressed by my wee ditties."

'Big Bill' from Cleit was Chief Scientific Officer to the Thatcher Government 1990-1995. Sometimes he's called Professor Sir William Stewart. He has three university degrees, and has been awarded twenty-three honorary degrees. He turned up to be interviewed with fourteen pages of hand written notes, a complete charmer!

## Siar FM
### Barra & Vatersay Community Radio

# Barra Island Discs

Janice's guest this week on Barra Island Discs is Bill Stewart from Cleat, a man who has a few letters to his name.

Listen in and hear how Bill aka Professor Sir William Stewart, originally from Islay married a Barrach and then went on to become founding professor of Biological Sciences at Dundee University ending up as Chief Scientific Advisor to the UK Government.

*Tune in to Barra Island Discs on www.siar.fm.*
*Monday, Wednesday, Friday and Sunday*
*3.30pm, 10pm & 4.30am (following morning)*

More information on Siar FM, its programmes and presenters including Janice Ross and Barra Island Discs, can be found at http://www.siar.fm

CHAPTER NINE

# Young, Daring and Bold

# *Young*

*Interviewed on 24.09.13*

Donald John Wilson – Deege

Life is for living and the exuberance of youth sparks brightly in Barra. It is highly contagious. Donald John Wilson, or Deege as he is known, is a cracking football player and beautiful young man. A few days before the cup final this is what he had to say.

"My mum's side of the family is Barraich and my dad is from Croydon, but my granddad is from Barra and my dad used to come up on holiday and met my mum. The rest is history.

I am still on a high that we have reached the final. I am massively excited because this will be the first one I have been able to play in because during the last one I was abroad, and the one before that I was injured, so I can't wait for this one. The final is Barra versus Iodchar Saints for the Billy McNeill Cup. Barra won it last year too because the goalie scored in the final minute so it makes it a bit special this year. People have been shaking my hand after last week. I think it was because I played well. The score last weekend was 4-0, we were playing against North Uist. I set up the first goal and then scored the third goal. I am loving it now, my confidence is quite high which is good for going into the final. It will be in Benbecula and we will take a forty-five minute ferry journey from Ardmhor to Eriskay and then another forty-five minute bus trip up to the Dark Island pitch in Benbecula and then we get ready to play. You can't sleep the night before, then the minute you wake up you are 'adrenalinated' and the hassle of travelling doesn't come into it.

I didn't start playing until I was eleven or twelve, but my Uncle Andy and my dad are really great at football. Both could have made it professional, but had difficult choices to make. My cousin Reece is playing professionally in Costa Rica right now, so there are a lot of us in the family who can play. There are lots of sports in the family. My other cousin plays rugby, so it isn't just football.

My dad comes when he can but he works at the airport. My mum thinks it is too brutal, and if I get tackled my Uncle Arthur [MacArthur] wants to come on the pitch and batter them, but it is all good. I am not big and the role I play suits me because I have to be fast and agile. A few people have said to me that I am a thinking player. If I get the ball I kind of create a dilemma for the other team. Some of them will have a go at me, but it is nice to think some of them are frightened of me. I suppose I am susceptible to tackling, and it is good because it means that they have to deal with you. I am never scared. You don't think about anything other than winning. You don't think about what they are going to do to you, you just think about winning, about how to position the ball and how to reach the best position to get to goals. It is having the mentality to think ahead."

Working together as a team is imperative to reach success and Deege recognises this.

"Since we have been playing the same eleven every week there is a continuity, we always know where everyone else is. I know where Screech will always be. Wowi is my cousin, and I know Liam and Sander from my class, and Craig Ferguson from school, and everyone else works in the community. There is a lot of support in the team. Nearly all the team lives in Horve so it is easy for training all week. It is really good. Our new coaches, Martin MacPhee and Andy McHardy, are really good. This is their first season and we have got a trophy already, and we are in another final. So it is great for it being their first season, and I love playing under them too. They make everyone happy at training. This is their first year with a new team. I haven't been involved before this year because I am still young, I am only seventeen. I am the youngest on the team.

I came from footballers in primary school where you can either play tig, or hide and seek, or football. I chose football, an easy choice for me really. It was just a game of football every break time. At secondary we started getting coached by Robert Ross and Tendai Mutambera who started teaching us fitness and strategies, and it became really serious but really good too. In S3 I started going to the seniors training, and it has been all up since then. Everyone else was a year older than me, but I didn't feel as though I was too young. It is just what I can do with the ball that is really important.

My dad's brother was a great player. He got scouted by Millwall, and after his first training session was hit by a car and decided against it. Anyway he is really rich right now so it doesn't matter, but he still has a hankering for football. People have told me a few stories of how they turned down their opportunity to play and then go on to regret it. When I was playing down in Sussex my uncle and that came along to see and support me. My cousin was doing a scholarship in America and he was in his second year when he was approached to go professional. He earns a good wage playing in Costa Rica. He is doing what he likes doing best, and he has found a girlfriend, got the football and money, so he has a lovely life. There are loads of opportunities in football."

I wondered if the opportunities included seeing the world and this is what he said.

"I am playing with the Uist and Barra Under Seventeens Select. It is made up of players of under seventeen level by Iain MacDonald and we have an under seventeen league. He takes the best players away to Sussex, to Holland, to everywhere. It is a great experience. I have been away four times. We just pay a small fee. I have been to Holland and Galway and Dublin in Ireland. I was captain last year in Dublin but we came in third. Last year we played in Galway. It was watched by thousands because we were on Irish telly. I was playing alongside two other Barraich as well, Neil Sinclair and Domhnall Ailean MacLean. It was so good that we got to the final even though we got beat. It was so good to be part of it. The mentality that we made it to the final was wonderful. It was the Umbro Galway Cup and there were teams from all over, teams from Israel, and Manchester United were there too with professional youth teams.

It was a pleasure to be in their presence and they were really good guys as well off the pitch, so it was just such a great experience. The professional teams, Man City and Man United, they had their Under Nineteen teams playing with them so they could get more experience of playing. They were in a different group from us but it was a privilege to watch them and I do think the Uist and Barra Select could have taken them.

These teams from the city with all the facilities, and here we are a wee team from the islands playing against them and beating them. I felt really good. I was captain because I was the most experienced player there and the manager believed I had the best ability. It was a great honour to be asked and I had the support of the guys on the team. Considering I was the only one from Barra in the team, and the other ten from Uist, and they still supported me, it gives me a massive confidence boost. When I came back from Dublin I went straight into the Barra team and I scored a hat trick so I was just booming with confidence. These trips last for a week and it is constant playing for a week - four games in two days. Then you would go swimming at other times. On each day the level of fitness definitely improved, it was like a massive work out. I play any sport and I participated in other sports. I am really good at all sports – not boasting, it is just that I am."

Maturity and calmness are qualities associated with the best football coaches, Deege is no exception.

"When I got into coaching, it was the young ones on the island who came to me and asked me if I only played football, and I said no. I feel like a kind of role model. They think football is the only world out there, but I tell them there are other sports to be involved in too. I am a football coach to the eleven to fifteen years old, and I take them every day after school. It is great because I get about twenty five kids coming along. I just pass on the skills my old coach Mr Ross taught to me, and I am just passing them on. And then I am sure one of the boys coming up after me will keep it on. I have awards for volunteering and I have a big CV of awards. The young ones look up to me and I feel as if I am a teacher. They all wait for me, so if I do something good they will all do it, and if I do something bad – but I wouldn't do anything bad, I am not that type of person.

We got ten footballs from the Barra Senior football fund and my old coach, Mr. Ross, got fifteen balls from someone who was giving them away. It is really good because I have the support of other people throughout the islands. The kids all tell me how they are going to play for Barra. They were there on Saturday, and when I scored they were all roaring. It was great and I could hear my wee brother.

I have an older sister at university studying Sports Science. She wants to be a teacher, and she is way too smart for me. And I have a little brother, Matthew, who looks up to me as if I am his hero. He tries to wear the same clothes as me and comes to the football. I don't treat him any differently, but it is lovely having a wee brother, brotherly love – but we do squabble. Matt is ten and he is showing promise as a midfielder.

I am an attacking player and I have a free role for Barra. It is good to know that I can do that, and the manager and coach, Andy and Martin, know where to play me. I am not a striker, I am a number ten. I go about and assist in the scoring, but I feel better setting up for other people. I like the feeling of having created the goal, and everyone is happy, to be honest. I am an unsung hero. Mr. Ross and Mr. Mutambera always told me I had to play in an attacking position, and to stay up the pitch. It is obviously a quality I have, and I am glad that they noticed it and they helped me. For a defensive player you need a bit of bulk. I don't have that ability to make slide tackles and that. I am fast over short distances. I don't like running for long distances. Mr. Ross and Mr. Mutambera's running drills were terrible, they just about killed me. So they used to just push me to run and the longer you went the faster you became. I am faster with a ball than some people are without a ball, so it is a good skill to have, it is good to know I have it for my position.

I cannot wait for Saturday and there is a supporter's bus going over from the island. A lot of people have told me they are going over, so it will be really good. All my coaching boys have told me they are going over, so it will be a really good game. It is amazing how much support we have. The same people are there cheering people on. You can't come to Barra without seeing the team. The tourists come to see us and they love it too. I am sure there are lots of young boys coming up who can fill my boots, they are so young but very talented.

The path to the Dark Island is opening up for me and I have travelled quite a distance in playing football."

Deege Wilson was not chosen to be in the opening eleven of the Billy McNeill Cup at the Dark Island pitch in Benbecula.

Barra lost.

Football in Barra has had a hugely successful year, becoming Hebridean team of the year 2015. Congratulations to all involved.

Deege Wilson

James Davidson - Team Captain. 2015 Uist and Barra League winners,
Western Isles Co-op Cup, Cal Mac Cup

# Daring

*Interviewed on 22.07.13*

**Catriona Nicholson**

Dancers are born with a grace and poise that cannot be taught. Catriona Nicholson is proof of this. She flits and floats like a butterfly touring the world. This is what she says.

"I think there is only so much teaching you can do with dancers then it is something which is inside, a certain spark. It is the same with actors, it has to come from the heart. Since about the age of two when my mum took me to my first competition I went home that night and tried to do the Sailor's hornpipe and an Irish jig. So yes I have always danced. I am quite petite and it is how we are.

I am a Barraich. My dad is from Bolnabodach and my mum from Tangusdale. My mum is a MacNeil and I am more of a MacNeil than a Nicholson. I think when we come from Barra we all have a spark, everyone from Barra has something special within them to give to the world. I think we take the beauty of the island with us around the world, wherever we go. I think the Barraich are everywhere – New Zealand and Canada. I don't think you ever forget where you have come from. It is the wonderful sense of community you have here, and the beautiful scenery. There is just something wonderful in us all.

I went away in 2007 for about four or five years. I took a year out and went to Australia and that opened my eyes to what I wanted to do and I came back and did a course in Outdoor Education. I finished my degree last year. I was a year in Glasgow and a year in Penrith down in the Lake District, and since then I have just been fumbling along enjoying myself.

Leaving school at seventeen, I found it hard to make the decision of what I wanted to do. I have found my way and I am

171

happy. The outdoors is your playground when you are living on an island, walking the beaches and cycling the roads, running up the hills, and that is outdoor education at its best. I think I was doing it, I just didn't realise how much I loved it until I left the island, and that's what I wanted to teach others. A lot of kids, even in Glasgow, have never ever been to Loch Lomond which is just an hour's drive – it is on their doorstep – but may not have the access, not have the money. So being in a position where I can take people outdoors is just great, especially if it is their first time. It is a really, really rewarding job. It is a job to build self-esteem, especially with the bad boys. It is about building confidence and team building, so it is very rewarding."

Wanderlust to see what is beyond the island's horizon keeps Cat moving on. When she told me she was a woofer I was waiting to hear a bark!

"I am staying on the island for a while, in a wee caravan beside the house, but we bale out when the wind and the gales blow through. It is lovely being home for winter. The colours of the island are just beautiful. Walking is very refreshing. I think my plan is to go away travelling with Ben Hartley and go to South America, then do a ski season in Canada, so we will just go out and see the world. When I am travelling I teach people how to ski, how to kayak and whatever comes up. I don't have a lot of money and I will probably have to get a job as a waitress in a bar, or anything. I am flexible and I might be a shepherd if need be. It is called woofing, working on a farm abroad or something like that, I think. I would like to learn loads of different skills and bring them back to Barra. Woofing is big in New Zealand. They will pay for your food and accommodation, you will probably not get paid for doing the work, but it is the experience isn't it? It is not like being a sheep dog. Basically it is cheap labour they are getting from people who want to experience what life is like working abroad.

In South America I want to do some mountaineering and go

to the Rainforest, and get some surfing done as well. There's lots of good surf out in Peru and Central America as well as Honduras and Costa Rica. It all sounds so tropical and luscious, just fantastic really. It started when I went to Australia after leaving school. It made me hungry for more. I think people say they haven't got the money, but then you have to prioritise what you want, and if you give up going out to the pub you can soon save enough to go a trip round the world."

Catriona Nicholson

Never having travelled further than Paris, and even then only for a coffee break, Cat's circumnavigation of the globe was making me feel dizzy.

"I think for my generation travelling has become more accessible with flights around the world being advertised everywhere. Lots of retired people do round the world trips. Ben's mum and dad are retiring this year and planning to do a tour of Europe and then go to New Zealand. They have the get-up-and-go too. I have met a group of friends and new people. You meet up with people again and again. When we were in Australia in a car park after a day's surfing, another van parked beside us and it was Nick and his girlfriend whom we had met in Indonesia. So it is a very, very small world. We hadn't planned to meet, but that is the beauty of it. Other travellers become like a family to you. And yes we do run out of money and you call home. My dad helps out and we get jobs as a bar help, but you just get on with it. You need to be careful and keep your wits about you. You learn and grow from each new experience. I send emails quite a lot and Skype is good."

Brotherly and sisterly competition on the football field is a joy to behold!

"My dad is a builder, in fact my dad is everything, just a happy go lucky kind of guy. I am the youngest of three – Mairi who is in Barra, Domhnall who is an engineer at sea – he loves it and he has just sat his next exam to become a second mate. He is a really good footballer. There are a lot of talented players in Barra. The girls played too. I don't know if I was that great a player. I think we were very lucky at coming into secondary at the time of having a female football team. Hella Bickle and Geraldine Circus helped us train every Tuesday and Thursday after school to help us enter the Coca-Cola Cup in Inverness. We got to play against Under-Sixteen teams that were around Scotland, so what an experience, you know. Without them it would never have happened. I think there was a history of women playing on the island, but not for a while, but some of the older women played, like Mairi Tinnan and Florag, they all played football. After I left school I played in Glasgow for a while. I had a trial for the Glasgow Ladies. I didn't get in but I hadn't practised for a while. A couple of summers ago we started women's football which was great. A couple of older women came along, it was for fitness and for fun. It is good because it challenges that stereotypical view. Football is not a man's game. It is a sport that everyone can play. I was always a tomboy and always, always encouraged to play football. I didn't like pink or anything. I was always covered in mud. I think my upbringing definitely shaped me. I am the opposite of the butterfly dancing, rather feeding me raw meat before the game. My dance teacher hated me playing football, but we loved sport and we couldn't let down Hella."

Catriona Nicholson is somewhere in the Canadian Rockies dancing round bears.

# *Bold*

*Interviewed on 19.05.11*

James Davidson

James Davidson is one of five brothers who play for Barra football club. He is captain of the team and knows they are on a winning streak.

"Barra FC has a really young team. Every other team keeps saying that. Hopefully if we keep the same team for the next couple of years we will start winning things. We have changed our management, Ally Eoin has left us. Tendai is focusing on improving our fitness because in the past, in the last half hour of the game, we would all tail off and the other team would score loads of goals. But now we are working all the way to the end, challenge other teams a bit more and pick up some more points.

At first I was chuffed being asked to be captain because there are older people in the team than me, but I don't really think about it. I just do the same thing and that is shouting abuse at people. Well if people, if the management think I have good leadership skills, then that is great. It is really encouraging. Wee Deege, he is only fifteen and in third year, and he gave their defence a lot of problems. It is a good encouragement for all of us, and everyone played really well. It is a good stepping stone for next season. If we take into next week the good points of the game, we will win. We want match reports in the *Guth* whether we win, lose or draw. I think it helps the team and the community to gather support.

My whole family has always been interested in sports, not just my brothers and the five of us who play, but my cousins as well. I am probably related to seven in the team. It is good to play with your brother because you know where he is going to play. That is good because you can anticipate where he will be on the park. I am second. There is Michael first; then me; then Steven; then the twins, Sander and Liam, and they are pushing to get into the team, but I am the tallest. Screech that's Stephen's nickname, is wee and nifty. Everyone one of us gives it their all.

Our team formation is really difficult to get because some of the guys have to go back to work as merchant seamen. The guys who are here all the time are either too short or too young, so it is changed every week. Iain Nicholson is an excellent goalkeeper and used to play with Oban Saints, so it is good and he can teach Neillie Boy some tricks.

In last week's game, Benbecula, in the first half, were one nil up but we managed to regroup, and we did it even though it was just a minute to go. Iain Eosa [Campbell] was my 'man of the match'. He was really good all day and didn't let them get away with anything. He set up the winning goal by preventing Benbecula from scoring against us. He played it down the line and wee Neil Sinclair managed to get the goal in. It was great.

I try to tell the boys to stick to black boots and forget the colourful ones, leave them to the professionals. But they like the colours. Deege Wilson is really fast and turns so quick on the ball."

When James is not lighting up the pitch with his dazzling team formations he is lighting up the island.

"I work with Hec Maclean, the electrician. I am going away to finish my final exams. I might have to move off the island to get some work. I might like to go away to work on the rigs. The way things are, work is really slow, but I don't have to keep pestering Hec for my wages. I didn't always want to be an electrician. I wanted to be a joiner, but I left school too young and there was no one here on the island to teach me. So I started working with Seonaidh MacLennan and I got my machine digger's ticket with him, but when I was eighteen Hec actually stopped me and asked if I wanted an apprenticeship. It was really good of him. I have been really lucky because I don't really want to go to sea. Sometimes they are away for months at a time and I don't want to miss the summer and that. I like Barra.

I joined the Lifeboat about eighteen months ago. I just go out on exercises, and in the summer there are call outs for yachts, so we do exercises in preparation for emergencies like man overboard and that. We need more women because there is only one woman with us on the crew. It is a good laugh because we all know each other. You kind of need sea legs but the adrenalin would stop seasickness I am sure. It is a really good thing to do.

I am one of five boys. Everything is a competition. It is who can shout the loudest, and my mum…I don't know how she puts up with us all. I couldn't sit there with six women. It is difficult. My dad and Alexander support Rangers, but the rest of us support Celtic, so we have quite a lot of discussions and it usually ends up with money being waged and hands shook at the end of it. It is all just banter, but in Glasgow it is sectarian. I think here on the island young people are not sectarian, but that is a generalisation. I don't really know the ins and outs of it. Here everyone pulls together. It is just like one big happy family.

At the time at school I didn't really enjoy it, but now think it was really funny. It was a great crowd and we were always getting up to something. I think that is the way it is supposed to be. Daniel and Bod are at sea, Seonaidh is a chef in Glasgow, Maria was a joiner for a while and Arlene is a social worker. I don't think too far ahead like winning the lottery. All I think about is next weekend.

I always came to Barra before I moved up. I lived in Fort William for most of my childhood, but I came here primary six or seven. I remember my mum telling me I was coming. I was so delighted. I don't have fluent Gaelic but have a few words and can understand the bodachs who I just smile at. I am having too much fun just now to think about classes. I am involved in Badminton, as a family we are all involved in it.

I play golf but there are not enough people playing golf on the island. The last couple of years it hasn't been busy. The greens are at a good standard, so I am trying to get people to join in. I hope Barra and Vatersay stays the same."

Every Saturday Captain Braveheart aka Jamesie leads Barra FC to victory.

## CHAPTER TEN

# Midwife
# Mother
# Matriarch

# *Midwife*

*Interviewed on 02.02.10*

**Nellie MacArthur**

Three things distinguish Nellie MacArthur from the rest of us. One, she has been in every nook and cranny on the island, two she is a wonderful teller of very funny stories, and thirdly she has been the island midwife for nearly 40 years. Casting a beady eye over life like the wise owl she is, this is what she says.

"I came to Barra in 1975 to visit a friend, Margaret Pisaneschi, who was here with her husband Eldo Pisaneschi who was teaching at the school. Margaret and I trained together as midwives in Glasgow, and after they had been abroad doing VSO they settled on Barra. I came up to visit and fell in love with the island on that very first visit, and you couldn't keep me from it after that. I was up every weekend walking around the beaches and climbing hills, I was younger and fitter then.

At the bottom of the gangplank I met my future husband. He was sitting on a bollard on the pier, and I asked him where I would get a bus to St. Brendan's. He nearly fell into the sea laughing. 'There is no such thing as a bus here.' It was not love at first sight, no.

I have four children, two lovely daughters and two lovely sons. My eldest daughter, Naomi, lives and works in Glasgow in a rehabilitation centre in Bridgeton, and helps people with mental health problems. My eldest son, Aaron, is fishing and enjoying that although he doesn't want to do that for the rest of his life. My second son, Caillean, is in fifth year at Castlebay Secondary school. He is a bit unfocused in what he wants to do with his life, but I think I was a bit like that at his age too. Grace is in school at Castlebay. Yes I have a handful. It is challenging. I think it is important to foster independence. In fact it was probably another ageing hippie saying to me, *what you give your children is roots and wings man, roots and wings,* and I think that is true. Children have to know where they belong and feel secure enough to spread their wings and fly free.

World peace is very, very important to me and I spent many days of my youth on demonstrations campaigning for nuclear disarmament. On one memorable occasion I went to Greenham Common Peace Camp where women were blockading a nuclear facility. I have been carried off the road on too many occasions because I want a world that is safe for my children and I want things to change. War should not be part of our lives. Being a midwife I feel the wastefulness of war and the impact of death and destruction on motherhood. I think you feel all the hard work that goes into having children, it is all so wrong, it is wasted for no purpose. Political purposes. Well, I will shortly be of pensionable age and I am full of plots of what I might do in the future when I retire. I was looking at protestors up trees and in tunnels and thinking I would have time to do that, but maybe not. My rheumatism would stop me getting underground!"

Story telling, like Nellie's midwifery, was born in Glasgow.

"Once upon a time I was a staff midwife at the Southern General hospital, and I was a bridesmaid at a friend's wedding. My hair was quite long and I wanted it curly for the wedding. So stupidly I went to a friend's brother's salon on a Saturday afternoon, always a mistake. Sure enough, I had the perm but it didn't look quite right when they had rinsed off the perm lotion. When I came out of the salon I put a scarf on to travel home on the bus. When I got home and took the scarf off my hair came off with the scarf. By this time it was Sunday and there was no-one open to fix it. I certainly didn't look like Sinead O'Connor, however much I wanted to! At the same time I had liberally slavered my face with cream to get rid of spots, and of course I was allergic to it as well, and my face was like a big red tomato with furrows of skin coming off. This was all because I had taken a wee notion for one of the young doctors at the hospital, and you know, with a smooth complexion and curly hair he might be interested in me. Another instance of leaving the potion on for too long. I thought I will need to get my head tattooed a colour, so at the end of each day I did that. Then next day was the

Nellie MacArthur

Barrathon and one of the raffles, which I won, was a shampoo and set! It was quite a long time before I could take them up on the offer because I didn't have any hair to be shampooed! Yes, down through the years I have had many adventures with my hair, with or without it.

There is going to be lots of different chapters in my book when I get down to writing it, and there is going to be a whole chapter about canines and their many forms I met on my travels as a nurse in the city of Glasgow. I can remember two you might find amusing. I will miss out the one that says on no account put anything through this letter box especially your fingers – that was in Govan, so I didn't. I opened the letter box to see why and there was this terrier at the other end of the hall slavering and getting ready to attack the post man!

I will tell you a story about when I was working in Priesthill. I was covering for a colleague, and she said to me, she warned me, 'Now look, when you go to this close beware of the dog. There is a problem with the dog in this close.' I thought right, I am warned. I have steel toe caps on my boots and I will watch out for the dogs. This was before the days of secure entries and I just went in. On the ground floor there was a small terrier, a Jack Russell, which flew out and attached itself with its teeth onto the small corner of my midwifery bag. I was shaking my bag and trying to batter it off the wall – please don't call the RSPCA! Then it detached itself. By the time I reached the next floor, where there was a gate across the landing which said Beware of the Dog, and two Doberman Pinchers were behind the gate, barking and leaping off this gate, I was thinking *good, God!* I ran up the stairs and collapsed against the door I was visiting, totally relieved, and chapped on the door. The door opened and there's this wee thin man in a vest, a bit like Rab C Nesbitt only half the size with braces, and at the end of the hall there was a German Shepherd dog with its ears flat down and its nose wrinkled and its teeth slavering and this wee man said, 'It'll no touch you, hen!' I said, 'It looks as if it intends to touch me with its teeth.' By that time the dog had launched itself forward, so I just shut my eyes. The dog leapt and went over my head, and I am not small. It grabbed my hat and landed on the landing. I slammed the door shut and the man in the vest said, 'Satan's no usually like that, hen, he's usually so welcoming!' The poor dog, with a name like that how else could it behave!"

Another story of her travels round Glasgow.

"The robbers of South Nitshill, my own patch. Well, I was on the bus, and there was always old ladies on the bus who just couldn't sit there. They would move about all the different seats. The bus stopped, and a man with a balaclava and what one can only assume was a sawn off shotgun and a plastic poke got on the bus. There was another fellow with him, but I can't remember what he was wearing, and he said to the driver, 'Take me to such and such.' And this wee aforementioned granny, who was sitting now in the front seat, was staring at the robber's feet, and she said, 'Hello James. What would your granny say if she knew what you were up to this morning?' 'Oh hello Mrs. McClements, I'm awfully sorry.' The bus stopped, and off they got and hared through the back courts. We all had to stay on the bus and give statements to the police. The robbers were recaptured, I think in about twenty five minutes. Nobody uses the number thirty nine bus as a getaway van I don't think!"

Nellie's hands have brought generations of Barra children into the world and after nearly forty years this is what she says.

"I always regard myself as an immigrant here, and while I love and appreciate and value the community, I am not born and bred to Barra. I am a transplant who has been lucky enough to be welcomed and to be a bit useful too. I am not a natural linguist and I have struggled to learn Gaelic. Despite taking classes I am still only able to talk to my dog who ignores me. The Gaelic language is particularly beautiful with its music and culture.

I have been made very welcome here in Barra and Vatersay and I am very privileged to have met so many wonderful people in their homes, and really do appreciate that I have been part of some very intimate moments in their lives.

Time changes you, and time changes everything."

Flapping her wings Nellie MacArthur is preparing for take-off.

**Beach runway on Barra**

# *Mother*

*Interviewed on 08.11.11*

Nanag Gillies is as much Vatersay as the white sands. Smoking and laughing a lot she is a formidable woman. It poured shamelessly the day of the interview but her sunny disposition brought a warmth that enveloped both of us. Here is what she says.

"I hope everyone enjoys this interview. Well, I was born in Glasgow in August 1937. But I was only a fortnight old when my mother died. And I was brought up then in Caolas on the island of Vatersay by my mother's sister and her brother – none of them were married. They brought me up as their own so to speak. That was the only mother I knew was her, but I knew she wasn't my mother, you know.

My father was in the Merchant Navy until he came home to look after his own parents. He was just next door to me. Well, my father and mother were from Caolas and they had a croft there. Well, it's been there since my granny and grandfather left Kentangaval and went over there at the time of the raiders – The Vatersay Raiders[1]- although they weren't from Vatersay! They left Kentangaval to go there, to Caolas, as did my father's people who came from Glen. They moved over there as well at the time of The Vatersay Raiders. It was 1910 they went there.

The Department of Agriculture took over the land when the Raiders first came from Mingulay. They raided the place.

---

[1] After 1850 when crofters had been evicted to make Vatersay a single farm, owned by Lady Gordon Cathcart, a series of land raids by people from Barra and Mingulay took place. These raids culminated in ten men, known as The Vatersay Raiders, being imprisoned in Edinburgh in 1908. Such was the national 'stooshie' about this, the government were forced to buy back the land and allocate it to crofters. However the wheels of bureaucracy turn slowly and it took 3 years before those from Mingulay were given land.

They built houses for themselves on the land. And they were imprisoned for it. After that, the land was divided into crofts so they could have their own potatoes and vegetables. And they could have a cow or two. And they had their milk when the cow was at milk during the summer. And they made their own butter and crowdie and that was it. It was a hard life! They did their own hay, no hay came in from the mainland then. They grew their own corn for the cows for the winter feeding and all that."

Reflecting back on her school years she remembers the journeys.

"I went to school in Vatersay. There was no road then. It was just a track road. Nothing but puddles! You would have to jump on stepping stones going across the puddles but we got used to it. But most of the days we went across the hill, straight up as the crow flies, down to the school on the other side, and the same coming back home.

We were taught in Gaelic. We had no English when we went to school. The teacher we had at school, she was English speaking. She was Irish. And I don't know whether she had her own Irish Gaelic. But I don't know how we were communicating with her. But anyway we got there and we learned English. We weren't taught in Gaelic, but when we were older we went to her husband. Her husband was the teacher in the other room. He was the Headmaster. When we went to him we started learning the Gaelic, but by then we were too old, whereas nowadays the children start learning the Gaelic when they're wee. All of my own children can read and write it apart from me.

Well, when we left there we went to Castlebay School - the Secondary School. I was twelve then. And we had to stay in lodgings, we only got home at the weekends.

There was no regular ferry nor nothing, but everybody practically had their own boat. You know they could take us over to Castlebay. And if it was a stormy weekend we would be stormbound for the weekend. We wouldn't get home.

It was hard! You were in other people's homes. You felt, you know, that you were in the way, especially when they had visitors coming in for a ceilidh at night, you know. You felt that you were pushed out, 'Go out and play.' Whether you wanted to go out or not, you had to go when you were told to go out and play. I stayed in lodgings in Nasg, I had three lodgings, two in Nasg and one in Horve."

I wondered what kind of difference the causeway made to her life.

"I never thought I'd see the day when there would be a causeway going over there. That made a whole lot of difference to the island. Vatersay is no longer an island so to speak. You had to go over to Castlebay in a boat to get your shopping from the shops and cart it up from the shore home, which wasn't easy either. You know there was hardly any landing stages there, jetties, proper things, but we managed. But the shop keepers were really very nice to us. You would phone - there was a kiosk and you could phone with your list of messages and give them what you wanted. They would send them over on the ferry, when there was a ferry. A ferry did start eventually. But first of all there was no ferry. And if you ran short through bad weather you could go across the sound [of Vatersay]. I've been a few times across the sound and was dropped at the Nasg road and I would get a lift from there to the shops. I would do my shopping and I would get a lift back over to the end of Nasg Road and start climbing the hill with all your messages on your back in a piggy bag, your back full of messages, carted over to the other side. They then could come over and pick you up on the other side because it would be too stormy to go right round the point to Castlebay.

We got our meat from Oban. A parcel used to come every Saturday. There would be steak and mince, and sausages, and black pudding, and white pudding. It was a feast day. There was no fridge, nor anything. We just kept it in the coolest part of the house which was the porch near the door. There was cupboards there, there was no 'sell by date' nor anything on it. We just ate it and it didn't do us any harm. It did us the whole week.

It is changed days now. But we had our own hens and our own eggs which was a big help too, and you know, when there was a clucking hen we would put eggs under her and she would take them up and there would be loads of chickens. We used to keep hens and cockerels. The weekend cockerels, well we used to kill them and put them in the pot and make soup.

Well, you couldn't buy eggs in a shop then. Some people would take a box in from their own, you know, if they had too much eggs in the house. They would leave them on the counter in the butcher's or somewhere in one of the shops. And if you asked for six eggs you would get six eggs in a poke and take them home carefully, you know, and that was it. I haven't had hens for years.

Nobody, nobody milks cows now. They just let the calf go with the mother. But at that time the calves were kept on a rope at the house, tied on the croft, and you milked the cows and you kept half the milk for yourself and the other half went to the calf."

Listening to Nanag's story I felt as though she lived a hard life. Here was her response.

"It was very happy times, yes. We were never away from the shore fishing for crabs, and fresh fish was so plentiful then. You could get fish just down from where my house is just now. That is more or less where I was brought up in the old house. And you would go down, just at the shore there, and cast the rod out and you would get fish, fresh fish right away. But not today, you can't get that. It's so scarce round the shores here anyway. It's very scarce.

The men, they started at the creels here after the war. They only had boats and oars with no sail or engine. When they started getting engines in the boat they were just going out… just a wee bit out with their creels. They would only have about thirty to forty creels and they would be full everyday! Lobsters were so plentiful. But then they had to pack them into boxes and put seaweed on them or something to keep them because they were going on the boat all the way down to Billingsgate in

**Nanag Gillies**

London. Sometimes in summer time, by the time they would reach their destination they would be dead."

When the time came to leave school I wondered if her hard life made her want to stay. This is what she said.

"I left school at fifteen and I started working in the priest's house in Castlebay. I was there for six months. It was very hard work! I have never worked so hard in all my life as I worked when I was in the priest's house! I stayed there but I used to get the odd weekend home. I used to be crying, 'I'm not going to go back there!' 'Oh, you'll have to go back! You'll have to go back.' So I did because I needed a reference. I stayed the six months then I went to Oban. I was working in a B&B in Dunollie Road with a Mrs Henderson. She was very nice. I stayed with her for three or four seasons. I enjoyed working with her, she was good! I liked her. I got on well with her.

I was working as a waitress, I quite enjoyed it. Then we used to go to Glasgow during the winter months.

I worked in the big houses down in Giffnock and Pollokshields. They were Jewish and they were very nice, both of them! Especially the Taylors who I worked with in Giffnock, it was just like being one of their own. They didn't keep me apart from the family. I stayed with them in the sitting room and watched television. Television was so new then to them, although they were well off. They only had got their first washing machine when I was there. And Fay Taylor, she was only twenty-eight. They were a very young couple. They weren't like the old fashioned Jewish families, but they always had the Friday special. They set the table with an extra place at the table on a Friday for the Lord coming.

They were a Jewish family. Well, I know that Fay Taylor, the wife, her people had a clothing factory. Oh I had beautiful clothes! Every month Mrs Taylor, Fay Taylor, put all her clothes to the jumble sale. But I had my pick of everything first of all before it would go. I had loads of lovely clothes; the same every month – I would get my pick. They were really very nice. They had two children; a seven year old in school, and the boy was four, and he was so small and so wee. I used to take him out in the pram on wet days, a big pram, an old fashioned pram in the garage, and he would say, 'After all Nan, sure I'm only a wee baby!' And then on nice days he was a big boy in a smaller pram. He was lovely! I was really sorry when I had to leave to go to the season again, back to Oban.

I had to go back to the season because you got more money in the hotels and you got a lot of tips. You got more in tips than what you got in a wage, you know! They were very good at leaving tips in Oban. Well that was it, we were never short of money!

Oh yes it was really good. We liked it in Glasgow during the winter months. You didn't feel the winter in Glasgow. You know, you were going to all the shops and all that. And it was quite sheltered. But when it came summertime it was too hot and too clammy, although I didn't like it when the fog was there, that smog, which was terrible."

It took marriage to bring Nanag back home.

"Well, I went back to Vatersay after I married in 1960. I got married in Glasgow.

My husband was from Caolas and we got married in Glasgow. I got married in Saint Mungo's. That's where I was baptised as well, in Townhead, that was where I was born in Southern Kennedy Street in Townhead. I came back to Vatersay in 1960 and I stayed with my auntie and uncle who brought me up for three years. By that time family had come along. I had a girl and a boy, and there was another one on the way and the house was getting too small. What with children and older people it just wasn't suitable. And so we got a caravan and we were in the caravan till the last of the family was born which was the youngest, Tony. I had eleven of a family and Morag, she died of leukaemia. I lost her at six and a half years of age with leukaemia. So they were all in the caravan before we managed to build a house.

It was quite hard but we got another one and they were joined together, there was two then joined together. We got our own generator, so we had electricity and I managed to get a second hand washing machine which was perfect! And we took the water home from the well ourselves with a pipe so I had the water in. You see, so it wasn't so bad then.

It was a twin tub washing machine, and of course there was no throw-away nappies then. No disposable nappies. It was terry nappies and they had to be boiled or they would be stained and horrible looking on the rope. So you boiled them in a big bucket, a galvanised big tub on the cooker on the gas until they were boiling hot and then you rinsed them out and hung them to dry in the breeze. The children grew. Youngest Tony he made his home over in Ireland. He's in Donegal, and Neil works down in Great Yarmouth. He was the second oldest. Ealasaid was the oldest, and Frances is just over there. I've got a daughter down in Eoligarry. She's married down there, and Iain, he stays down in Horve. He's got a house of his own there. And Joe he's in Northbay and he works in the airport. Is that them all?

Well Donald's in my father's house which he renovated. Donald is just next door to me at the back of the house. Flora she's in Callander. She works in the Edinburgh Woollen Mill. She's a manageress there and she's got one boy. He's twelve years of age.

When I had my children they were the happiest days, they were the happiest days. There was many a laugh, you know. It was one big lot of laughter with the children. I loved them! I used to read them stories and things like that and they used to sing songs and all these wee ones, the children, they loved that! It was good and it went past too quickly!"

Nanag's life seemed to have come full circle.

"I was quite happy. I'm quite happy. I've been over to Ireland to see Tony. I went over with Tony after he got married. They were staying in Killibegs in County Donegal. They're still in County Donegal but they've moved to Ballybuffey, it's nearer to the hospital where she works, that was the reason for their moving. Tony's at sea and he does a month on and a month off at home. He takes after his dad and granddad. My husband was at sea.

He was in the Merchant Navy from the time he left the school. He was still in the Merchant Navy for three years after we married. Then he came home and he got the job as school janitor and doing the conveyance for the school children. That kept us, along with cows and sheep, and we were all right! We managed to build the house anyway.

It was baking every day then, we baked scones every day instead of going to Castlebay. You would only get loaves every second day in Castlebay anyway. It was more or less what it is now. You can get loaves every day but you get the fresh ones every second day. It was easier to bake, that was it, you had to feed your family.

When I was growing up there was a shop in Caolas and there was a few down in Vatersay, but there's no shops there now.

I was also knitting, knitting and knitting and knitting, but I don't do much now as my hands are so bad with the arthritis. I knitted all the children's cardigans and socks and everything, even my husband would knit the socks for the children for he could knit as well! When they were young in school the boys they got knitting as well as cookery. I don't know what happens nowadays. The boys here I don't think get cookery or knitting or anything like that. Some of my knitting is still on the pins!

My life was just with my family. I was just at home in the land of the wee people."

Using the Vatersay pattern Nanag Gillies knitted her family together.

# *Matriarch*

*Interviewed on 17.09.10*

Patricia Buchanan comes from Ardveenish. She is mother to four. She is learning to drive. She writes down songs sung by the older generation so they are recorded for posterity. She is a grand singer herself and chose to sing some songs during the interview. She knows a few things about Barra. This is her story.

"I am sure I could put a few stories together if I remember them.

I live in Horve but I am originally from Ardveenish. I moved to Horve to have my children thirty-two years ago but I was born and bred in Ardveenish, in a beautiful spot. It is my father's house and my two sons are renovating the house, Michael and Raymond. One of my two boys works with the BBC, the eldest Michael works for the World Service in London. And Raymond works for the Weir Group in Glasgow. I didn't rule with the iron fist but I made sure they did their homework every day and every night and gave them as much encouragement as I could. That is how you get on in this world. They did very well, very well indeed.

My daughters are both nurses, Fiona works in St. Brendan's, she's my youngest, and Elaine my daughter is married up in Falkirk and works in the intensive care unit in Stirling Royal Infirmary looking after new born babies. That's quite specialist, it is a specialist nurse that she is.

I am very proud of all four of them, very proud indeed.

When we leave the island we are very naive, and when they left the island they were very young. They left at the age of eighteen and they had to go and meet other people, even live in other people's houses, renting out a place or have lodgings with other people. Mammy wasn't around the corner and it was very, very difficult for them, but I was always, always at the other end of a phone for them, if need be. The family I've got really get on well with other people, they mix well, very sociable and very friendly. They thought *this is the Glasgow people,*. But they always come back… three of them are married now, but they always come back, summer, Christmas, Easter, New Year, they

Patsy Buchanan and daughter.

always come back to Barra for their holidays.

I brought the four of them up on my own and I couldn't go back to work and leave them. There wasn't the child-minders that there is today, you had to rely on family or a friend. I have six grandchildren, two girls and four boys with the eldest being six years and the youngest fifteen months."

I asked her what her own life had been like.

"I left the island and worked in South Uist and then worked in Raigmore Hospital [Inverness], training to be a nurse. You know, a good laugh is the best tonic for all them patients, crack a joke and you will be fine and you'll be ready to be discharged the next day."

Buchanan is not an island name and she explained how it appeared on Barra.

"Buchanan originated from Skye. My grandfather came from Skye and my grandmother came from Bolnabodach and they met up and got married. My grandmother's name was Màiri MacNeil, so I do have the MacNeil roots in my blood somewhere. But that's how my grandfather came to Barra, he came to work here."

Choosing to sing herself in the studio, *Faillaidh o' lo'*, her voice brought a sweet resonance to the interview. She continued with this.

"Most Gaelic songs are love songs. It is about a young lad who has gone to sea and left his loved one behind him, but unfortunately he died and never came back. Most of the Gaelic love songs are about sailors and tragic accidents that happen to them. It is quite a nice song.

Chrissie Mary MacDonald from Eoligarry and I sang for years together in Northbay Hall. Many a ceilidh we sang at in Castlebay Hall, and all over the island as well.

I wasn't a professional singer, just an ordinary Gaelic singer from Barra, a traditional singer from Barra. Manys a time I sang over in Vatersay and over in Castlebay School with The Vatersay Boys.

I never entered the Mod, but I have been singing since the age of nine. I didn't have the confidence then…no…no…no. I didn't mind singing in Northbay Hall or something like that, but not the Mod. When I started singing there was no encouragement in them days you just sang, then you just sang in your own sweet way somewhere. When I was nine years of age I just started singing, I was at Eoligarry School then. It was the teacher who noticed a wee voice somewhere in the corner and I was asked to sing in Northbay hall at a ceilidh. There was plenty of ceilidhs in them times and I remember the song was *Jevan jevan jevan*, and remember I was only nine years of age. I was so smart, or at least I thought I was, and I sang one verse and one chorus, and half way during the second verse I couldn't remember the words and I just ran off the stage. To this day I have never sung that song again, it was just an embarrassment. It was very embarrassing for my mum and dad with me running. And not only that, I said to the audience, 'Well that's enough, you have had enough and I am off.' That was a bit cheeky for a nine year old.

The Mod wasn't so big then and there wasn't any financial help or anything. You just plodded along and that was it. My great auntie Mary Morrison was a great singer, so I suppose I got the music through her as well. She would have gone a long way if she was alive today, but she never got the chance, just like I didn't get the chance in them days."

Patsy's schooling meant a lot to her.

"My teacher and I meet occasionally when she is in Barra, Mary Katy Campbell from Eoligarry. I still see her about here. She taught me and Neil MacNeil, he is not with us anymore, God rest him, but they were my teachers. Then I moved from Eoligarry to Castlebay at the age of twelve. We used to travel by bus. I think I did well at school, I always wanted to become a Gaelic teacher. Again it happened because there was no money, no encouragement or anything like that, and you had to leave then at the age of twelve if you wanted to get further. My parents thought that I was too young to leave the island. I think lots of people lost out there. There was no sixth year then.

I was four years at Castlebay, and then I stayed on because I wanted to do another year in Gaelic. I was sent into the medical room in Castlebay and it was a one to one tutor, Ruraidh Campbell, he is on Barra now. He would give me homework in the morning. I used to sit there from nine to four doing homework, and that's what I got in my extra year, so there you are. Then I went to do nursing.

I can read, write, sing, and speak Gaelic, but I don't think I could go to college, leave the island at my age and go to Jordanhill College, I don't think so!

Gaelic is really, really important to me. I grew up speaking Gaelic at home and my children all speak it. Raymond doesn't write Gaelic, but Michael reads and writes it as well, and he tries to sing it but he is not a singer. Fiona is a beautiful singer but will not come out in the open about it. She loves singing, is a lovely singer, but she doesn't tell anyone about it.

I used to sing with Iain McLaughlin all over Uist, Eriskay and wherever he played, and that wasn't yesterday. Manys a tune Iain McLaughlin could play, he was a fantastic accordionist. I have been on the radio and the television that came to Northbay Hall years ago.

I used to sing with Fergie MacDonald when he came to do a tour of the islands.

I met him in Daliburgh Hall and I sang with him then, and I followed him all the way through to Barra then up to North Uist and Carinish Hall.

The thing is I don't like travelling. I don't like travelling in airports, I just don't like them. Barra to Eriskay, Barra to Oban that's enough for me. Glasgow to London, that's my limit. I just go to London to see my son and his kids. I don't go abroad, not at all. Although when Michael, my son, was working over in the States for three years with President Bush, I went to see him and his wife. I stayed in Maryland. I was there for three weeks. It was so beautiful over there, really nice. We went sight-seeing and all that. My first day I went to see President Bush, but he had heard of me and told me I wasn't welcome! We went out all the time. We went to New York, I preferred the states to New York because Times Square is too busy. Castlebay Square is enough for me!"

One of the reasons Patsy had been a target for an interview was she loved being among the old people, collecting all their songs and tales told in their own island way. This is what she said.

"I go to the Cobhair Bharraigh to see the old people and sing to them. I get songs off them and I write them down, then Morag Robertson or Maria put them in a folder for the next generation. People do remember, I just jot them down as they remember them. Being able to write them down is good. They are in their heads, really old, old songs. I love the old people. You and I will

Above – Patsy Buchanan surrounded by her nine grandchildren at her father's croft in Ardveenish which her two sons have done up for her.

Below – Patsy Buchanan with three of her family.

be going in there next, Janice, if we remember where the building is! They sing verses of beautiful Barra tunes and one day I sat there with an old man and wrote twenty six verses of a song, verses that – he is not with us any more – would have been lost. I wrote them all out. It is great and they do like to sing it especially if I know the tune. They will sing it and it is absolutely fantastic. I start the tunes and they give me the words and I write them down."

The thing about Patsy is you can't talk to her because she makes you laugh so much. We laughed like drains throughout this interview, except for when she was singing her songs, it was deadly serious then.

She has since passed her driving test.

# *Afterword by Janice K. Ross*

Everyone has a story to tell. Barra Island Discs allowed the community of Barra and Vatersay to tell theirs.

The life-stories of those I have interviewed are all unique. The focus of the show has been to fundamentally share life-stories with a local audience. In my interviews I have tried to convey a sense of the uniqueness, the individuality of each person's life and their contribution to the island community. What is collectively poignant about them is the sense of occasion they created for both me and those involved. There was an intimate atmosphere and sense of trust created as soon as they entered the studio. I can appreciate that people entering a new social space can feel uncomfortable, but the laughter we shared about life's ups and downs erased any awkwardness making it a really special experience. It was people bearing their souls to the island through me, telling me things that they had never had the opportunity to tell before. During the musical interludes I have been given tremendous insight into hidden stories and was told a few secrets about the island, all of which will stay secret with me forever. Listening figures suggest we have a global audience but it is the Barra and Vatersay community which has been the focus of Barra Island Discs. This book is the intimacy we shared in the setting of the local community radio in downtown Castlebay.

I am not really sure how it took off but within a few months Barra Island Discs had become a feature of island life. The local paper *Guth Bharraidh* [Barra News] helped to generate interest. A weekly preview column featuring a photograph of the guest taken in the radio studio was accompanied by a short synopsis of the show's highlights. For some the photograph and its appearance in the *Guth* was a 'worse' fate than the interview itself! In fact Sir William Stewart (or Big Bill the crofter) told me the reason why people came forward was because they wanted to appear in the *Guth*! I am not entirely sure if everyone would agree with that! The show has given me a unique insight into this small Hebridean community on the edge of the Atlantic Ocean. What a great opportunity to combine getting to know people as well as recording their voices for historical and cultural purposes.

When, a number of years ago, my husband took a job in the Highlands, our first move as a family was from Lanarkshire to the village of Glencoe. We left behind us the coal-bing scarred landscape of Cambuslang, to settle in the cool, clear, crisp mountain air of Lochaber.

Moving home for me was a real temperature drop, even sitting in front of the open fire I was chilled and one day while I was serving teas and coffees at the Glencoe visitor centre, I found myself agreeing on the phone to cover a supply teaching post on the island of Benbecula. Thereafter I came to Barra.

I love Barra's landscape: its miles of sandy beaches teeming with dancing oystercatchers and jigging sanderlings; the fulmar and guillemots nesting on ragged cliff faces and gannets arrowing into the furious sea. I love the surging beauty of the ocean, and its ever changing melody.

Island life for me creates a warm glow inside that no dram or roaring fire can match.

Janice's family rolling eggs at Easter

# *Acknowledgements*

My grateful thanks go to the following-

Those associated with Siar FM – Murdo MacNeil, Seumus MacKinnon (jingle!)

Voluntary Action Barra and Vatersay past and present - Jessie MacNeil and Maggie Dewar/Eoin MacNeil and Annie Gillies

Dr. Sabine Dedenbach Salazar Saenz and Alison Scott of Stirling University

Robert (proof reader), Madeleinea, Kathleen, Patricia Claire, Donald, Leah, Theo and Calum Robert MacNeil - what a bunch x Barbara Drummond, Domhnall Uilleam MacLeod III MBE, Curstaidh Peigi and Mary Catherine for translating into Gaidhlig, Nicola Hoarau

Jules and Lizzie Akel - you know what you did x

Dorothy and Russell Bruce of Twinlaw Publishing

All those who gave up their time to be interviewed and whose stories make up this volume

Moira Baird for her wonderful map and AnnieM for sourcing it

**Photographic credits:**

Rory MacNeil of Barra, Bernard Anderson, Nick Brannigan, Rob Brett, Sheena Beaton, Joanna MacLean, Mike Shailes, Michelle Galbraith, Patsy Buchanan, Flora Campbell, Non Campbell, James Davidson, Dol Mickety, AnnieM, Chris Close for Christopher Brookmyre, Norman MacLean, Peigi Townsend, Sandy Maciver for Donald S Murray, Roddy Mackay for Billy McNeill, Allan Milligan for Angus MacNeil MP, Elizabeth MacIntosh, Naomi MacArthur, Stephen Mairi Wilson, Ben Hartley, Christine Galbraith, Rachel Biddy, Donald Manford, Malcolm MacNeil, Tom Paterson, Sandy Ferguson, The Screen Machine, and the delectable Meg Rooney for The Vatersay Boys at The Ferry 2015

Moran Taing.